RE-CHURCHING

THE UNCHURCHED

GEORGE BARNA

ISSACHAR RESOURCES
A DIVISION OF BARNA RESEARCH GROUP, LTD.
VENTURA, CALIFORNIA

Published by Issachar Resources, a division of the Barna
Research Group, Ltd., 5528 Everglades Street, Ventura, CA
93003. All rights reserved. No portion of this book may be
reproduced, stored in a retrieval system or transmitted in any
form or by any means - electronic, mechanical, photocopy,
computer scan, recording or any other - except for brief quotations
in printed reviews, without the prior written permission of the
publisher or author.

Library of Congress Cataloging-in-Publication Data
Barna, George
Re-churching the unchurched / George Barna
Includes bibliographical references.
00-108712
ISBN 0-9671372-1-7

Printed in Canada

CONTENTS

ACKNOWLEDGMENTS

Although I write every word on every page, writing a book is never a solo effort. Many people work behind the scenes to make such an endeavor possible. I'd like to briefly but sincerely thank many of the individuals who facilitated the birthing of this book.

Our friends at the North American Mission Board (NAMB) of the Southern Baptist Convention have consistently focused on reaching the unchurched. They graciously allowed me to use portions of the research that we conducted for them – and that they paid for – in this book. I am grateful for their generosity, for their partnership, and for their modeling service to the kingdom. Any interpretations or statements in this book do not necessarily reflect their position or views.

My colleagues at the Barna Research Group not only worked with me to gather the research data on which this book is based, but to also free me from the tyranny of running the operations of the company. I am especially indebted to David Kinnaman, who has helped bring the company to a new level, largely without my interference. Rachel Ables somehow managed the editing, design, production and distribution of this book while also juggling all of our seminar and resource marketing activities. The rest of the core team provided invaluable assistance in this and the myriad of other projects in which we were also involved: those teammates include Chris Daradics, Kristen Daradics, Pam Jacob, Jill Kinnaman, Carmen Moore, Sarah Polley, Irene Robles, Celeste Rivera, and Meg Wells. I have been blessed with a young, talented, and vision-driven team that is contributing value to the kingdom.

I am grateful for the editing assistance of Julie Carobini, too. Someday I will learn the rules related to hyphens and semi-colons. But not this week...

I appreciate the perseverance of Kim Wilson, who directs the activities of The Barna Institute. In spite of my consistently ignoring her while I wrote this book, Kim kept the wheels rolling with energy, joy and wisdom.

As always, my family has made the greatest sacrifices during this time of writing. My wife Nancy played every role during this burnout period, doing the home schooling, cooking, house cleaning, taxiing, playing, Bible reading, praying – you name it, she master-minded it in order to free me up to prepare this resource for the Church. My wonderful daughters, Samantha and Corban, regularly checked on my progress and prayed for me (and with me) every day. There is nothing as encouraging as having a loving, caring, supportive family; I thank the Lord for providing me with one. And I pray that He will repay them for their sacrifices.

Thank you, each of you listed here, for your blessings to me.

And you, reader, can make it all worthwhile by taking the information contained in this book and using it to bless people, to fortify the Church, and to honor God. I wrote it for you, for that purpose.

One

The Crowd Waits For You

Do you have a favorite passage of Scripture? Mine is the closing portion of Acts 2, which describes the beginning of the Christian Church, just after Pentecost. Every time I read that passage I cannot help but wonder who would *not* want to be part of such a community of faith. I am convinced that if the typical unchurched person were invited to get involved with such a collection of people, engaged in the kind of life described in those few verses, they would jump at the chance.

And why shouldn't they have the chance? God created us to be involved in such a church. Jesus died so that we might have the opportunity to share that kind of experience. The Holy Spirit was given to us to foster such a dynamic and transforming vehicle for ministry. All of Heaven is pulling for us to "do church" the way in which the Lord intended. Our hearts naturally yearn for such a spiritual family on earth.

So what will it take for us to get from here to there? What will it take for us to enfold America in God's designated entity for spiritual development and nurture?

I believe the answer relates to commitment. It will take a true commitment to God. It will take commitment to a vision of how each of us might truly be the Church, not just attend one. It will require a commitment to love and serve all people. It will take commitment to using our gifts and resources to develop a living body of believers that is indistinguishable in essence from the church described in Acts 2.

Are you willing to make such a commitment? This is not meant to be a rhetorical question. This is big – a big vision, a big promise. Let me explain what I think we're facing if we say "yes" to such commitment.

COMMITMENT TO GOD

So much of the pain and hardship we endure from day to day could be alleviated if we truly devoted ourselves to knowing, loving and serving God, and to living in the ways He prescribed in the Bible. The Bible cautions us that we will never alleviate societal problems such as poverty and hunger, nor will we escape the consequences of our humanity (emotional distress, physical pain, bad choices, etc.). But, some would say, if we had a more appropriate perspective on life, we would experience more of the joy and blessing that God desires us to experience. Right? How amazing it is that two-thirds of all Americans think that the purpose of life is to enjoy this reality and gain the maximum fulfillment from its options and temptations. God's plan is clearly different. He hopes we will become single-minded about life, fully focused on Him. But we have become distracted. In fact, the growth of the American economy is largely based upon developing distractions – newer, bigger, better, more sophisticated distractions. He allows it, but He is not honored by it.

The first step toward truly preparing to reach the unchurched is for you to become a living representation of His intended Church, a one-person model of faithfulness, obedience, holiness and righteousness. God's Church is not about structures and systems and resources; it is about people. It is about you and your relationship to God. When that relationship is in order, it will affect the people around you, whether you want it to or not.

One of the most impressive things to me about religious leaders known throughout the world is their ability to influence people who do not even know them personally. Mother Teresa affected people that way. If you watched her, talked to her, or just hung around in her presence, her passion for God and her determination to live the way He called her to live rubbed off on you. For some people it caused them to be excited about the possibilities, for others it created internal guilt regarding the gap between them and God, for yet others it generated a desire to reflect more deeply on life's meaning and potential. Billy Graham has the same effect on people.

Have you met anyone like that in your life? You love to be around them because they have something that is attractive, something that is different but compelling.

The key question is this: as a believer in Christ, why aren't you and I that kind of model to everyone we encounter? That's what God had in mind.

As you ponder ways to approach the unchurched people you know, think about the nature of your own commitment to God. Our offer to the unchurched ought not to be that they join an organization, or that they hang out with a nice group of people. The offer ought to be that they, too, can have a relationship with God that will restore in them the same thing that you experience and that you have become. Jesus expressed this when He said to His disciples "follow Me." What the unchurched must do is follow Jesus – completely, unashamedly, joyfully, willingly, longingly. And for that to happen, you must show them the way.

If we are honest with ourselves, part of the reason why many people remain unchurched is that they have looked us over and don't especially like what they see. Some of us talk the faith but don't live the faith. Others don't even talk it very well. Maybe we've never thought of ourselves as hypocrites, but here's a test: How many people can we name who have re-examined their life because there was something in ours that they saw and craved but did not possess? That something is more than just having said a prayer to determine your salvation. It is a continual awareness of, and response to, the presence of God – a spiritual, emotional, intellectual and physical transformation accomplished by giving the Holy Spirit free reign in your life, resulting in an entirely new way of being God's Church on earth.

Our research is clear on this point: many people name Jesus as their savior, but relatively few have lives that consistently demonstrate He is truly the Lord of their heart, mind and soul. Perhaps before we invite other people to take part in the things of God we should commit ourselves to fully experiencing all that is available to us through Jesus. When that happens, we won't have to worry too much about attracting and assimilating others into the church. When God becomes the true priority in our life, and we imitate the heart of Christ and live in the power of the indwelling Spirit, what we represent will be irresistible.

Two

Sizing Up the Unchurched

Cross-cultural studies have consistently demonstrated the religious bent of Americans. Compared to people of other countries we are more likely to believe in God, to pray, to own Bibles, to give money to religious organizations and to attend church services. Ask the people you meet on the street about their religious convictions and you'll find that more than four out of five will describe themselves as Christian and most of them have some sense of the basic lessons and principles taught in the Bible – even though they may not believe them or live in accordance with them. America may not have a great memory for its own history, but one of the enduring qualities that defines the nation today, as it did back in 1776, is its appreciation for religious freedom and involvement.

But there is a story within a story here. Yes, most Americans call themselves Christians and most are willing to associate with some type of Christian church, be it Protestant or Catholic. But the moral and philosophical ambiguities that have reshaped our culture in recent years have affected our religious perspectives and practices, too. Being "Christian" has lost much of its meaning in this age of relativism, tolerance, diversity, ecumenism and syncretism. To say that Americans are a people of deep faith because of the breadth of religious activity is about as intelligent as claiming that we are the healthiest people on earth because we eat more pounds of food per capita each year.

Consider, for instance, what people mean when they say they are "Christian." Overall, this term has become a generic description meaning that the individual believes in a universal deity (generally labeled "God") and would agree that there was historical person known as Jesus Christ, who was a great teacher and miracle worker. To be Christian in America indicates that you probably own a Bible, attend church services at least occasionally, and believe that religious faith is at least somewhat important in your life. The significance of that faith is manifested by regular engagement with God through prayer, belief in the power of angels, and the contention that involvement in some faith system is better than faith abstinence.

However, although most Americans say they are "Christian," they do not necessarily mean that they have any type of vital relationship with Jesus Christ, or that they believe that their eternal outcome depends on Jesus. A minority of people in America are born again – meaning that they have an ongoing, personal relationship with God through Jesus Christ, that they have confessed their sins to God, and that they believe they will live with God for eternity solely because of the grace extended to them through that relationship with Christ. The number of people in the U.S. who are *not* born again Christians is somewhere in the neighborhood of 180 to 190 million people. If that group were a nation unto itself, it would be the third most populated nation on the planet, behind only China and India!

There is another significant group, though, that we must consider – the group that will be the focus of this book. Those are the unchurched Americans – people who do not attend a Christian church, in spite of the presence of 324,000 Protestant and 20,000 Catholic churches throughout the nation. The unchurched population varies in size from year to year, but it generally encompasses about one-third of the adult population and slightly less among young people. In mid-2000, we estimate that about 95 to 100 million Americans of all ages are unchurched. (We define a person as unchurched if he/she has not attended a Christian church service at any time during the past six months, other than special events such as weddings and funerals.)

To place that population size in context, if all of the unchurched people in the U.S. were a nation of their own, they would be the eleventh most populated country on earth. Only Bangladesh, Brazil, China, India, Indonesia, Japan, Mexico, Nigeria, Pakistan, and Russia would have a bigger head count. They would have triple the number of people that currently reside in California. It would be like having thirteen New York Cities (all five boroughs) combined.

Clearly, the religious nature of America has not affected the life of every person in the same way. And for nearly 100 million of our fellow citizens, the church is not part of their life. For those of us who are outreach-oriented – and that should include all who call Jesus their savior – reaching those people with both the good news of the grace extended to them by Jesus and the benefit of being part of His Church is one of the greatest challenges we will face in this life.

GETTING CLARITY

Penetrating the unchurched population may require a different approach than you might normally have taken. This book is based on two years of research conducted with several thousand unchurched adults and teenagers randomly selected from across the country. As I will try to explain through the statistics and the extended interviews we conducted with these people, in many ways they are very similar to you and me, but they are significantly different in some important ways, too. The same strategies and experiences that may have encouraged us to become involved in the life of a church may have no relevance to the needs, expectations, aspirations and lifestyles of the unchurched. We will have to be discerning and wise as we approach them – never compromising what we stand for simply to attract numbers of people, but never losing our compassion for them either.

Some of what you read in this book will come as a surprise to you. Other facts and insights will confirm what you have experienced or suspected. To set the stage for a deeper discussion of the many insights we have gained into the minds and hearts of the unchurched, let me summarize some of the important "big picture" insights that we will dissect in greater detail in the chapters that follow.

→ As the new millennium opens, there is great interest in returning to the Christian Church. Many individuals whose past affiliation with churches was only marginal, or was not fulfilling, are seeking a deeper faith connection and are open to integrating a faith community into their lifestyle. Many of them, however, don't know where to start: they are both bewildered by the massive array of choices, yet mostly ignorant of that full range of options and the substance of those places.

→ Unchurched people cover the spectrum of people groups in our society. If we study the averages, we find them to be pretty typical of the aggregate population in terms of age, marital status and regional location. However, the unchurched are more likely than the population at-large to be male, to have experienced a divorce, and to have greater education and income than the norm.

→ One of the important revelations in this research is that unchurched people are not "people persons." They tend to be more combative, less relational, lonelier, and less flexible. They want a church that is a caring community, but they are not especially willing to bend over backwards to fit the relational style of a congregation.

→ Don't assume that the unchurched feel they need God because they are miserable. More than average, these are people who are aggressive, high energy, and driven. They have made something of themselves, by the world's standards. Their hard-charging lifestyle has left many of them frazzled from stress and broken relationships, but they do not necessarily believe that God, Jesus, religion, the Bible, faith or Christianity will help them overcome the struggles they face. They are open to the possibility, but not predisposed to believing that the answer is bound to be faith-based.

→ The reasons why these folks avoid church can be viewed from two different angles. On the one hand, we can point out that they do not attend churches largely because they don't think it is worth the time and effort. On the other hand, given their vulnerability to faith inputs, we also know that a huge explanation for their absence from the church is that they have not been invited to participate. The chances of them coming on their own, without soft but continual encouragement from trusted friends, is slim.

→ The initial means to attracting the unchurched is through invitations to events rather than pressure to belong to groups, and via personal relationships more than media marketing. The approach must be personal, but not high pressure, entertaining yet relevant and substantive. Expect them to resist highly-polished marketing efforts; they are skeptical of institutions and marketing, in general, and slick religiosity, in particular. (Caution: Do not confuse "slick" and "excellent.")

→ There is not a single one-size-fits-all strategy that will unlock the gates to reaching the unchurched. Like everything else in our world these days, attracting this population will require multiple strategies, inherently consistent with each other, undertaken simultaneously. The most successful marketing strategies, though, will be sensitive to the needs for control, perceived value and a personal touch.

→ Just as political campaigns use imagery, symbols and terminology to signal their heart, so must the faith community utilize such tools in communicating with the unchurched. Among the substantive hooks that will speak positively to these people are the notions of compassion to others, applied faith principles, healthy families, love of children, genuine interpersonal caring, efficient use of time through the delivery of relevant substance, integrity, authenticity and personal experience.

→ The components of each unchurched person's "dream church" varies. In general, most unchurched adults are seeking a church of 100 to 200 people; a casual atmosphere; a place demonstrating reverence for God; the integration of meaningful traditions; practical, topical preaching; and other features that are customized to the needs of the individual.

→ The unchurched are quite focused on the matters that they believe to be important. Example: God is vitally important, but the church is not. Another example: being Christian matters, being born again does not. Naturally, these perceptions can change, but be aware of what you're up against from the beginning.

→ Most unchurched people are open to involvement in a church, but they are not actively seeking such involvement. They tend to be worldly first, spiritual second.

→ A small but significant proportion of unchurched adults are born again Christians – almost one out of five. If churches understood these people better, this group would be a natural segment to attract back to the church. Bringing back this group alone would swell church attendance by more than 15 million people – which, if evenly distributed across the nation's 350,000 or so Christian churches, would equal more than 40 new people per congregation. That inflow would constitute the largest return to the church during any decade in the past century and would increase the size of the average Protestant church by almost half!

→ Churches across the nation are experiencing tremendous success at relating to the unchurched. However, there is not a standard formula or program that invariably works among the unchurched. Getting to know them intimately and then designing relational strategies around their needs and aspirations makes all the difference.

That's just the beginning. Let's dive into the discoveries we've made from our research among the unchurched. By better understanding this important group of people, we can better serve their needs and honor God.

Do you want to see the lives of people changed by the power of God, and converted into positive energy for the purposes of His kingdom? Are you looking for ways to minister with impact among a group of people who are spiritually confused and may not even realize it? Would you like to see the Christian Church in America, and your home church in particular, explode with new participants who are hungry for a taste of genuine truth and significance? Have you watched in dismay as the morals, values and lifestyles of our nation have decayed, wondering what you could do to help bring about a moral and spiritual revolution that would improve our society and its peoples?

If you answered "yes" to any of these questions, then read on. God is calling you to represent Him in the lives of a nation within our nation: the unchurched of America.

17

Three

WHY PEOPLE AVOID THE CHURCH

On the face of it, given who the typical unchurched person is, staying disconnected from a church makes no sense. Most unchurched people think of themselves as Christians. Most of them own Bibles, the very book that describes the importance of being connected to God's chosen ones in a true community of faith. Among the greatest needs of Americans these days are the desires to feel relationally attached to other people in their midst, to find the answers to life's big questions, and to make a difference in the world – all life quests that the church exists to facilitate. One of the greatest concerns among U.S. adults is the deterioration of moral values – an issue of paramount concern to Christian congregations. And one of the greatest personal needs among millions of people is for their children to have a well-rounded, positive, moral education. Once again, the church would seem to be a natural option for people to turn to in this regard.

Yet nearly one hundred million people live without a connection to a faith community. Spiritually activating and guiding those people is one of the daunting challenges of the age. It is a God-sized challenge that demands tremendous faith, courage and determination – and reliance upon His Holy Spirit for the wisdom and tools to get the job done.

Undoubtedly, the first step in the process of connecting with the unchurched is to pray for the tools and the opportunities to influence those lives for Christ. A reasonable second step would be to figure out why such massive numbers of people are avoiding a connection with a church.

From the start we should be clear about something: about half of the unchurched adults were formerly churched people and the other half have never had consistent exposure to church life. There are two interesting facets to this.

First, when we conducted similar research 15 years ago, we found that the number of unchurched adults who had previously been churched was much higher than it is today. In the mid-Eighties about four out of every five unchurched adults had been churched at one time. This radical shift is largely a consequence of the fact that a large proportion of Baby Boomer parents broke with tradition and did not bring their kids to church much. Many of the Boomers who did give their kids exposure to church life did so inconsistently. The consequence is a large portion of people within the Baby Bust generation who are completely or mostly lacking in church experience.

The second important facet is that half of all unchurched adults have made a conscious decision to dropout from church life. Reconnecting those people with a local church will typically require us to address their past experiences before they will seriously consider re-engagement with a church.

REASONS FOR DROPPING OUT

There are several ways of gaining insight into the reasons behind the absence of the unchurched. You can ask them what they liked least about their church experiences, assuming that their disappointments and frustrations drive their choice to avoid the church in the future. Alternatively, you could ask them why they have decided not to attend a Christian church. We asked both of these questions and received answers that were similar, but with some important nuances to consider.

When asked to describe what they did not like about their past church experiences, there were three common answers. The first was that they disliked the hypocritical behavior of church people. "They get all pious and religious on Sunday morning, but they forget about their religion the rest of the week," was a representative assessment provided to us by one of the unchurched women we interviewed. The alleged hypocrisy of church attenders was especially bothersome to people in their fifties and beyond, and among divorced adults. About one out of every five unchurched adults found this contradictory behavior to be problematic. (See Table 3.1.)

A second aspect that many of the unchurched deemed repulsive was the strict and inflexible beliefs of the church. "They tell you what you're supposed to believe – they don't leave any room for discussion or interpretation," explained one disenchanted former church regular. The types of people most upset about the theological rigidity of churches tend to be those who earn above-average incomes and residents of the western states. Again, one out of five people listed this as a reason for their failure to make church a part of their daily regimen.

The third common answer, also given by one-fifth of the unchurched, is that there is nothing in particular that they disliked about the church. To these people, the church was simply not compelling. "Look, if you want my time and energy, no problem – as long as you deliver the goods," warned an unchurched Boomer from Missouri. "I went to a church for years, but never got much out of it. After a while you figure there's not much to be gained by that affiliation. I hate wasting my time, there's too much to experience in life. So I've moved on."

Naturally, other reasons were given, too. One out of every eight people said they did not like the way the church worshiped. One out of every ten felt the church was too focused on raising money. Smaller numbers of people listed reasons like the feeling of superiority conveyed by the congregation, the pressure to join or to return, and being told how to live.

TABLE 3.1
WHAT UNCHURCHED ADULTS LIKED LEAST ABOUT THEIR PAST CHURCH EXPERIENCES

(N=230)

Hypocritical behavior of the churched	21%
Strict/inflexible beliefs	21
Nothing in particular	21
The worship service (long, boring, etc.)	12
Too much emphasis on giving money	9
Air of superiority among the churched	6
Pressure to join/return to the church	4
They tell you what to do/how to live	4

When we asked unchurched adults to describe why they currently do not attend a church, the top-rated reasons were that they were too busy to do so (or had scheduling conflicts), that the church had nothing of interest to offer, or that the individual was just not interested in being involved in a church.

These reasons describe the reticence of almost half of the unchurched. The life stage of respondents was clearly related to their answers. For instance, parents of kids under 18 were the most likely to say they were too busy for church. Senior citizens and those with college degrees were the most likely to say that the church has nothing of value to offer them. (Table 3.2 shows the replies people gave.)

A sizeable segment (one-seventh) responded that their religious beliefs differ significantly from those of the church crowd. This was most common among Baby Busters (i.e., those under 35 years of age) and among upscale adults (i.e., people earning $75,000 per year or more, and those with a college degree).

These particular protestations are not surprising. Busters, many of whom possess postmodern perspectives and others of whom have crafted unique theological views, are notably sensitive to belonging to groups that demonstrate ideological tolerance and embrace the notion of diversity. In fact, a recent study we conducted among teenagers showed that young people increasingly feel comfortable with substantive contradictions while feeling limited by rigidly consistent frames of thought. Meanwhile, upscale individuals tend to be less concerned about tolerance, but quite confident in their own intellectual abilities and conclusions. Blanketly accepting the "party line," no matter who the party may be, often does not sit well with these individuals.

About one out of every eight unchurched people write off the church because they do not believe in organized religion or in the necessity of worshiping God through a church experience.

The remaining reasons each represent relatively small segments of the unchurched. For instance, only 4% say the beliefs of churches are too rigid or inflexible. Three percent mentioned that they dislike church people, or that the church is only interested in their money. Each of the following reasons was named by 2%: they don't believe in God or Jesus; they had bad past experiences in church; a physical disability precludes their attendance; they haven't found a church they like; they are held up by family issues; or they are not a religious or Christian person.

Don't overlook the fact that 15% say they do not attend church but they don't know why. Qualitative research we have conducted in the past has shown that most of those people, when pressed, simply have little interest in, or have not felt a need to get involved in a church.

Did you notice the extraordinarily small numbers of people who avoid church because they don't believe in God or in Jesus? Or the small number who contend that the church is too money hungry to justify their presence? Or the relative handful who have been chased away by bad past experiences? How affirming and encouraging it is to find that people tend not to avoid the church for "irreconcilable differences."

What are the obstacles we must overcome? The major considerations are indifference and value. Millions of the unchurched don't care about church involvement because they don't see any need to get involved. Millions more stay away because they cannot make the value equation work: that is, when they calculate the amount of time, money and energy they would have to invest in the church, they do not see a reasonable return on the investment. Unchurched people, like most Americans, are practical individuals. They do not get excited by promises perceived to be unrealistic ("this church will change your life" or "you will never feel more loved than when you become part of this fellowship") or by extensive religious programs. They want personal benefits that they understand and desire. Most of the unchurched figure they've gotten along just fine without the church for a long time, and until someone gives them reason to feel otherwise, they will remain spiritually unattached.

TABLE 3.2
THE MAIN REASONS WHY PEOPLE
DO NOT CURRENTLY ATTEND A CHURCH

main reason for not attending church	2000	1990
no time; schedule conflicts; working	26%	24%
not interested; nothing to offer; no reason	16	16
my beliefs are different than the church's	14	9
don't believe in organized religion;		
don't need to worship at a church	12	8
their beliefs are too rigid/too inflexible	4	*
dislike the church people; they're hypocrites	3	2
the church only wants my money	3	2
don't believe in God/Jesus	2	2
had bad experiences at church in the past	2	2
physical disabilities prevent going	2	*
haven't found a church I like	2	*
family considerations/disagreements	2	1
I am not Christian/not religious	2	*
dislike denominations/denom. churches	*	6
churches are irrelevant to my life	1	5
other	5	5
don't know	15	22
sample size	831	406

(* indicates less than one-half of one percent)

A DECADE OF CHANGE

Take another look at the data in Table 3.2. The table contains not only the reasons why the unchurched stay out of churches in mid-2000, but also the reasons that were given by the

unchurched in 1990. What changes took place in the inter-
vening ten years?

Very few, it seems. The main reasons why people fail to
go to church stayed the same, as did the proportions of people
who listed each of those reasons. In fact, the two lists bear a
striking similarity from top to bottom. You might conclude
that the psychological obstacles to reaching the unchurched have
changed little in the last decade.

There are a few minor shifts that reveal an important
pattern, though. Notice that three of the five most commonly
cited reasons for remaining unchurched were more likely to be
offered in 2000 than in 1990. The thread that ties those three
items together is that they all relate to the penchant for
personal expression, independent thinking and the adoption of
diversity and tolerance as a philosophical mantra. With
postmodernism and even nihilism becoming more prevalent in
our culture, the trend toward rejecting absolutes and
uncompromised principles continues to gather steam. Here,
again, is a contradiction: unchurched people desire experiences
that are substantive, helpful and efficient, yet they reject the
foundations of one of the world's most proven, time-tested
solutions to their needs simply because it seems inflexible and
unyielding.

The decline in the percentage of adults who do not know
why they avoid church is also noteworthy. As noted earlier,
although many of those who cannot articulate why they remain
distant from the church are actually indicating that the church
has failed to provide them with sufficient value, the decline in
the "don't know" response is partly a reflection of people taking
the church more seriously as a lifestyle option these days. A
decade or two ago, most unchurched people had pretty much
made up their mind that church was not in their future plans,
end of story. Today, however, with the moral chaos, loss of
personal vision, search for meaning and pop culture fascination

with spirituality, the church is not as easily dismissed as an alternative. Many adults who are presently unchurched arrived at that state after serious consideration of the value of church. Their conclusion – "no, but thank you" – does not minimize the fact that they were (and many remain) willing to consider personal involvement in a local faith community.

So What?

One creed of the unchurched must be the well-worn Clint Eastwood line: "Make my day." If that day is to be Sunday, you make it worthwhile for these outsiders by providing perceived (and delivered) value. What you provide may well have to be a multi-faceted value product: part spiritual, part relational, part practical, part entertainment. Because so many of the unchurched are not born again, and therefore have no real relationship with Jesus, attracting and retaining these folks will take more than a good worship service, since the very practice of worship is outside their frame of comprehension and experience. They need a solid worship-plus experience.

To provide what the unchurched are seeking will require you to walk a fine line between what they want and what you can provide without losing your character. For instance, we must walk the fine line between providing them personal benefits without compromising biblical truths and traditions. We must walk the fine line between giving them what they deem to be of value but without promising more than we can realistically deliver or delivering more than we can theologically justify. We must walk the fine line between being open, loving and accepting, yet staying firm in our spiritual convictions.

Keep in mind that attracting the unchurched is not solely about marketing. Take another look at the reasons why they don't go to church and why they left church in the first place. No amount of clever marketing is going to overcome boring or endless worship services, the negative impact of hypocritical congregants, or the tedium of "business as usual" at the church. There must be a genuine and authentic expression of God's love, God's truth and God's vision for these outsiders to want to become insiders. Marketing may get them in the door once more, but they'll flee faster than a bullet train if they sense that the church they've returned to is the same church they left some years ago.

While you're examining the tables that describe what they do not want to experience in a church, read between the lines. Clearly, they are not looking for an institutional attachment. Translation: they are not looking for an organization or group to join. Even the Busters and Mosaics, our two youngest and most relational generations, are not seeking the church as a social vehicle. Also, the unchurched are not quietly asking for a guilt trip related to their rejection of God, His people or His events. Making them feel bad for shirking God and providing a pat solution (i.e., "Come join us as we gather together to celebrate our relationship with Him.") will do more harm than good.

A final word of caution is in order regarding the implementation of whatever strategy you deploy for reaching the unchurched. The data tell us that the reasons why they stay away don't change much over time. We're in the midst of the fastest moving period in American history, a time when our society re-invents itself two or three times a decade – yet, the reasons why the unchurched reject the church remained consistent in the last ten years (at least). If you develop a viable plan for reaching and connecting with the unchurched, and it doesn't all fall into place as quickly as you had hoped, don't rush to scrap the plan and start over. Give your well-conceived strategy time to work its magic. Better yet, give the Holy Spirit time to work through you and your people in your honest efforts to build relational bridges to the unchurched. Time is of the essence, but frantic and constant revising of sound strategy is foolish. Get a strategy you're comfortable with, undergird it with prayer and superb follow-through, and trust God for the results.

Four

A DEMOGRAPHIC PROFILE OF THE UNCHURCHED

You use demographic information all the time. When you interact with a person in their seventies, you probably don't bother talking about the latest rock music or Veggie Tales videos, because you know it's not relevant to them. When you go out to lunch with a college student, you probably don't wait for them to pick up the check, knowing that their budget is limited. When you visit friends in California, you are likely to avoid talking about hurricanes (since they don't have them), but you might discuss earthquakes.

All of these choices you have made are predicated on demographic knowledge. Demographic characteristics are common background traits, such as a person's gender, age, income, education, gender, region of residence, or racial heritage. Because such attributes are based upon stable conditions (i.e. you can't change your gender and your age progresses in a very predictable manner) rather than variable conditions (e.g. your attitudes about life or your hopes for the future), demographics become a very useful tool for understanding today's conditions and predicting tomorrow's probabilities. But as we intuitively realize, those traits may also enable us to have greater impact upon a person or group.

For instance, we know that people who make more than $100,000 annually are less receptive to potluck dinners or home visitation than are middle-class or working class people (although nobody is terribly excited about either of those strategies anymore). We know that women are more interested in relationships and in ministries that connect people than are men. We know that Baby Busters are the generation most likely to reject sermons that tell them what to do. They prefer stories and questions that challenge what and how they think, offered in a non-judgmental manner. These are just a few examples of demographic insights that can be translated into effective ministry strategies.

There are exceptions to every rule, of course, but when you are striving to craft a strategy or plan for effective ministry, those approaches will be most effective if based upon factual knowledge about the people whose lives you wish to impact. Demographic information is not the only body of knowledge that should be integrated into your strategies, but it is certainly a helpful building block within the process. With that in mind, let's examine the demographic background of the unchurched.

MEN DOMINATE

Men constitute slightly less than half of the national population, but they represent a slight majority of the unchurched (54%). Since 1990, in spite of the efforts of various ministries aimed at men, there has been an increase in the proportion of the unchurched who are men. (Imagine what the numbers might be if we had not focused on spiritually awakening the hearts of our men.) These data can be seen in Table 4:1.

TABLE 4.1
THE DEMOGRAPHIC PROFILE OF THE
UNCHURCHED AND CHURCHED POPULATIONS
(Base: adults, multiple national random samples combined)

	(N = 1507) Unchurched	(N = 1336) Churched
Gender:		
Male	54%	46%
Female	46	54
How many fit this age range?		
18 to 24 years old	15%	11%
25 to 34	19	17
35 to 49	35	33
50 to 64	20	23
65 or older	11	16
How many achieved these educational levels?		
High school graduate, or less	46%	46%
Some college, did not graduate	26	26
College graduate	28	28
Household income, before taxes:		
Under $20,000	19%	13%
$20,000 to $39,999	36	39
$40,000 to $74,999	26	30
$75,000 or more	18	18
How many fit these marital segments?		
Currently married	53%	57%
Have never been married	26	22
Currently divorced	13	12
Currently separated	2	2
Widowed	6	8
Have ever been divorced	31	23
Racial heritage:		
White/Caucasian	74%	70%
Black/African-American	8	14
Hispanic	11	12
Asian-American	3	4
Other	3	1
Have kids under 18 living in household		
	36%	32%
Region:		
Northeast	27%	19%
Midwest	20	24
South	27	37
West	26	20
Medians:		
Age	41 years	44 years
Years of education	14 years	13 years
Household income (pre-tax)	$36,697	$39,245

31

We can observe the data from a different angle to gain even greater perspective on this. Overall, almost four out of every ten men stay away from church, compared to about three out of every ten women. That may not seem like a big difference, but when you project it over the aggregate populations of each of these groups, the gap becomes enormous. If we assume that there are about 70 million unchurched adults, then we estimate that roughly 38 million of them are men and about 32 million are women. That gap of six million people is equivalent to the entire population of Massachusetts or Indiana.

In comparing unchurched men and women, we also discovered that the men were much more likely than were women to never have been married; were much more likely to reside in the South; and that there are twice as many non-white unchurched men as there are non-white unchurched women. Unchurched men were also considerably less likely than women to not be registered to vote. This is significant because it typically reflects people who are less engaged in society and relationships.

MOST UNCHURCHED ARE UNDER 50

While young adults have a reputation for comprising a disproportionately large share of the unchurched, that bad rap is somewhat misleading. It is true that they are more broadly represented than their share of the general population warrants – but not by as much as has been suggested. Adults between the ages of 18 and 34 – in essence, the Baby Busters – make up one-third of the unchurched, but slightly more than one-fourth of the churched base. At the other end of the spectrum are adults 50 and older, who represent almost four out of every ten churched adults, comprise just three out of ten unchurched people.

The median age of the two segments shows the difference between these groups from a different angle. The median age of the churched is 44; among the unchurched, it is 41. A gap of that magnitude is noticeable and statistically significant, but hardly monumental. (For instance, the median age of people who buy rap music is under 30; the median among those who buy classical is over 50. That's a gap that you can do something with!)

The median age of the unchurched has risen significantly during the past decade, from 35 years of age in 1990 to the current level. This indicates that as the unchurched segment continues to change, it is both keeping its base as they age as well as attracting an increasing share of people over 45 – especially among the older two generations (i.e. the Builders and Seniors). During the last ten years, the proportion of people 50 and older who are unchurched jumped from 22% to 31%. That rise compensated for the decline in the share of church absentees under 35, plummeting from 47% to just 34%.

EDUCATION IS THE SAME FOR EVERYONE

About half of the unchurched have gone as far as completing high school, one-fourth has attended college without graduating, and the remaining one-quarter graduated from college. The educational achievement profile of the churched population is identical.

THE CHURCHED MAKE MORE MONEY

The close tie between education and income, combined with the revelation that the churched and unchurched have virtually identical records of educational achievement, would lead us to expect the two groups to have similar household income levels. Such is not the case, however. Based on median household income levels, the churched earn about 7% more income than do unchurched adults. This is not attributable to differences in educational achievement, but it may be a consequence of the older average age of the churched.

What makes this small gap more significant is that the general demographic nature of the unchurched would lead us to expect the unchurched to have the higher average income. The larger shares of unchurched emanating from the Northeast and West, the higher proportion of men, and the higher percentage of whites – all of which are groups whose median income exceeds the national norm – would support such an expectation. But this is why we do research: to discover things that we did not know or did not expect, and to figure out what it means and what to do about it.

FAMILY SITUATIONS

The marital status of the two target groups is quite similar. Slightly more than half of each group is currently married (53% among the unchurched, 57% among the churched) and about one-quarter of each segment is made up of folks who have never been married (26% and 22%, respectively). The remaining one-quarter is divided between those who are divorced (about one out of eight), widowed (one out of every 16) and those who are presently separated from their spouse (2%).

Back in 1990, slightly less than half of all unchurched adults were married; a decade later, slightly more than half are married. The percentage of unchurched adults who has never been married dropped from 32% in 1990 to just 26% in 2000. Even so, the chances of being unchurched are much higher if a person has never "walked the aisle." Among adults who have never been married, close to half (44%) are unchurched – significantly higher than the chance of a married adult being unchurched (29%). In practical terms this means that unchurched adults who are married outnumber those who have never been married by a two-to-one margin, even though never-married individuals are more inclined to avoid churches. They are simply outnumbered in the population, which renders their tendency to reject church life less noticeable.

We also found that about one-third of all unchurched households contain children under the age of 18. If we explore the aggregate number of unchurched children in America, we estimate that figure to be in the range of 25 to 30 million individuals under the age of 18. Keep in mind that the youth segment is especially important when we talk about spiritual impact. A study we conducted recently revealed that if you calculate the probabilities of people accepting Jesus Christ as their savior, those between the ages of 5 and 13 have a 32% probability; individuals in the 14 to 18 age range have a 4% probability; and people between the ages of 19 and death have a 6% chance. In other words, we have the greatest window of opportunity for reaching people with the gospel before they reach their teenage years. The chances of seeing their life change spiritually after that point are relatively slim.

PROBABILITY OF ACCEPTING CHRIST AS SAVIOR

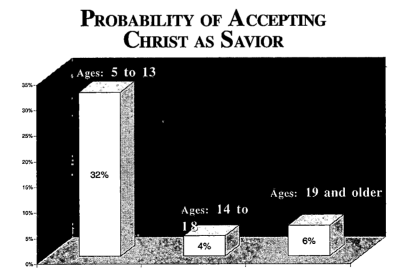

WHITES ARE THE MAJORITY

Abstaining from church life is less palatable to blacks than to other ethnic segments of America. Consider this: blacks constitute 14% of the church population and just 8% of the unchurched population. This is because less than one out of every four black adults avoids church. In contrast, slightly more than one-third of all white and Hispanic adults remain unattached to a church. A majority of Hispanics remains affiliated with Catholic churches – the only ethnic group for which a majority embraces Catholicism.

REGIONAL DIFFERENCES

The trends regarding geography are not surprising. The two regions that supply a disproportionate share of the unchurched are the Northeast and West. Those two regions together represent 43% of the nation's population, 39% of the churched total, and 53% of the unchurched body. In contrast, the residents of the South constitute 34% of America's total population, but they contribute 27% of the unchurched mass and 37% of the churched aggregate.

Given this, it's not surprising to learn that it's a lot easier to find unchurched folks along the coasts. In the Northeast (Maine through D.C.) 42% of all adults are unchurched. In the western and Mountain states, 39% of the resident adults have no church involvement. Those numbers are considerably higher than the parallel figures for the South (27%) and Midwest (30%).

SO WHAT?

Are you lost in the numbers? Let me free you from the tyranny of statistics: memorizing or even understanding any of those numbers will do you relatively little good. There is value to be gained from such demographic discovery, but it must be put in perspective. Here's a perspective that might be helpful to you.

First, keep in mind that the profile of the unchurched demonstrates that there is tremendous diversity among these people. There are many different types of unchurched individuals, and each one of them matters to God. Keep in mind that even the smallest demographic niche identified in Table 4.1 – for instance, Asians, who are only 3% of the unchurched – represent a huge number of people. (There are more than two million unchurched Asian-American adults, plus another million-plus kids.) Unchurched people are not all the same.

Second, the demographic diversity of the unchurched requires that we develop a wide variety of informed and intentional strategies for reaching them. This is not a one-size-fits-all group of people. We must wisely and purposefully target different groups through different forms of ministry. Penetrating the unchurched world requires us to be creative and savvy. Good intentions alone won't get us too far.

Third, the changes witnessed over time suggest that some formerly churched people become unchurched while some unchurched folks join the churched mass. This is to be expected in a fast-paced, change-oriented, highly mobile society. Yet, in spite of these fluctuations in who is unchurched, the most significant fact is that the demographic character of the unchurched remains relatively stable over time. This consistency permits us the luxury of creating long-term approaches to winning back the unchurched.

Finally, notice that the unchurched are generally similar in background to the churched. However, we know that their relationship to the church is completely different. This intimates that demographic information may offer some helpful bits of wisdom, but that demographics alone are probably not the key to reaching the unchurched. You may expect to learn some valuable lessons about those who reject the church, but the core revelations about what it will take to turn them into committed, growing and productive followers of Jesus Christ are to be found elsewhere.

With that in mind, then, let's consider another dimension of these people – their values, attitudes and lifestyles.

TABLE 4.2
THE PERCENTAGE OF VARIOUS SUBGROUPS THAT ARE UNCHURCHED
(N=649)

Population subgroup:	% who are unchurched	Population subgroup:	% who are unchurched
AGE:		**GENDER:**	
18-24	46%	male	39%
25-34	36	female	28
35-49	33		
50-64	29	**ETHNICITY:**	
65 or older	23	white	34%
		black	23
EDUCATION:		Hispanic	34
high school or less	36%		
some college/trade			
school	32	**HOUSEHOLD INCOME (PRE-TAX):**	
college graduate	32	under $20,000	42%
graduate studies	31	$20,000-$39,999	34
		$40,000-$74,999	28
MARITAL STATUS:		$75,000 or more	33
currently married	29%		
never been married	44	**REGION:**	
separated	36	Northeast	42%
divorced	34	Midwest	30
widowed	26	South	27
		West	39
HAVE KIDS UNDER 18 IN HOME:			
yes	24%		
no	35		

Five

VALUES, ATTITUDES, AND LIFESTYLES

To build bridges to the unchurched community, we have to understand who they are. Knowing their demographic background is of some help, but we need to know something more intimate about what makes them tick, or their spin on life. To get closer to the heartbeat of the unchurched, let's examine how they view themselves, their personality types, their political leanings and some of their common lifestyle activities.

HOW THEY SEE THEMSELVES

Psychologists and cultural analysts sometimes criticize surveys that ask people to describe themselves because, they point out, people often have a very skewed sense of who they are. Their criticism is correct. We all see ourselves differently than others see us, partly because we have a different understanding of what we're thinking and why we do certain things, and partly because other people observe us in certain situations and for limited amounts of time.

Despite this shortcoming, though, delving into people's self-perception gives us a valuable entrée into their life. If we know how they see themselves, then we can better estimate what types of responses they will have to various opportunities and challenges. Such insights make it easier for us to develop authentic relationships with them, to understand their responses to the world, and to provide ministry that meets real needs and issues in their life.

If you study the data outlined in Table 5.1, you will discover three things. First, there are relatively few dimensions on which the unchurched describe themselves differently than the churched. Second, there are relatively few extreme answers, which means that there is great diversity within the body of unchurched adults. Third, the unchurched portray themselves as aggressive, controlling individuals – again, not unlike most other people, but an important trait to keep in mind.

TABLE 5.1
HOW THE UNCHURCHED DESCRIBE THEMSELVES

	unchurched	churched
self-sufficient	94%	91%
like to try new experiences	81	76
like to keep things light	70	74
like to be in control of things	70	64
enjoy deep discussions	68	77
skeptical	62	57
avoid conflict whenever possible	60	74
financially comfortable	57	66
trying to find a few good friends	55	47
too busy	52	47
enjoy making tough decisions	51	53
searching for meaning and purpose	50	48
often misunderstood by others	44	32
in debt	42	38
stressed out	36	27
career comes first	33	16
dealing with an addiction	10	10
sample size	600	1402

Note that three of the most widely accepted self-perceptions are that they are self-sufficient, experimental, and controlling. Relate that to what we seek to do in our churches, and the kind of individuals we hope people will become (i.e. God-reliant, Spirit-controlled), and you can immediately see why so many of the unchurched have no interest in church involvement. As self-sufficient beings, they feel no compelling need to rely upon God for much of anything. As experimental individuals, they may well be turned off to the restrictions that Scripture and church doctrine place on various lifestyles, entertainment forms and relationships. The urge to be in control is difficult to satisfy in a church – either theologically (God is in control) or operationally (the system is in place and is hard to change – just ask church leaders). In fact, exerting control over your church experience is particularly difficult when you are an outsider coming in to a church; the prevailing wisdom among the faithful is that the church exists to change that person, not to be changed by the newcomer.

There are a few distinctions between the two groups that are worthy of comment. Notice that the unchurched are distinguished by being less likely to avoid conflict and to feel financially comfortable. In contrast to the churched they are more likely to feel misunderstood, to lack good friends, to feel stressed out and to place their career above all else. These traits do not describe all of the unchurched, but they begin to convey the impression that a sizeable number of unchurched people – at least in comparison to the churched – are driven, tough, perhaps even lonely individuals.

Do you know anyone like this? If so, you can imagine them explaining away their relational difficulties. "People have a hard time dealing with real leadership." "If people can't handle the truth, that's not my problem." "Explaining and enforcing necessary rules doesn't make you popular."

41

Many of the unchurched appear to be frustrated, as indicated by their high levels of stress, their confusion over meaning and purpose, and their admission that their life is just too busy. This irritation may also be fueled by the sense that in comparison to other people they are not getting ahead in life.

Now look at the figures displayed in the next table (5.2). This reveals a little bit about how they think of themselves in spiritual terms. The highest-ranked term – "theologically liberal" – is an expression that makes most Protestant pastors turn pale. Nevertheless, almost half of the unchurched describe themselves this way, as do one-third of the church attenders, but only 13% of pastors say that this term accurately describes their church. Almost as many unchurched people said they are theologically conservative as had labeled themselves liberal. Once again, a major divide occurs here between them and the churched (about six out of ten adopted the conservative label) and pastors (eight out of ten of whom said this accurately described their church).

TABLE 5.2
THE SPIRITUAL SELF-DESCRIPTIONS

	unchurched	churched	Protestant senior pastors
theologically liberal	46%	32%	13%
theologically conservative	43	58	79
a committed Christian	39	87	N/A
deeply spiritual	37	71	N/A
charismatic or Pentecostal	21	21	29
an evangelical Christian	12	51	83
sample size	600	1402	601

Not surprisingly, the unchurched were only half as likely as the church regulars to describe themselves as "a committed Christian" and "deeply spiritual." They were only one-quarter as likely to say they are an "evangelical Christian." The shocker was that both the churched and unchurched were equally likely to brand themselves as "charismatic or Pentecostal."

So, the portrait is being filled in a bit more. Now we can see that although they may think of themselves as religious people, most of them do not believe that they are deeply spiritual or that their ties to Christianity are anything more than nominal. A Christian church or group of people, therefore, is nothing special to them; it is one option on the religious horizon, but not necessarily a compelling alternative or even their first choice.

Continue to piece the puzzle together by examining the figures in Table 5.3. From this we learn even more about how they handle life. Again, three overview insights emerge. First, their personality profile is incredibly similar to that of the churched. Second, in comparison to the churched, America's unchurched adults appear to be less relationally inclined – just as the data in previous chapters indicated. Third, most of these people see themselves as competent, pragmatic, and capable of successfully interacting with people. They believe that their decision-making is more likely to be influenced by logic than emotion, but they perceive their choices to be a good balance of the two inputs.

Finally, consider the information provided in Table 5.4. This information is related to the personal style profiles originally developed by Carlson Learning Systems, who developed a self-administered test known as the Performax (or DiSC) profile. This inventory examines how a person relates to the expectations of others and to pressure, providing an index of behavior. No particular behavioral type is better than any other; the tool simply describes how a person handles reality. There are many variations on this profile that have been developed over the years, including the one we used in our surveys.

The information regarding the unchurched shows us that they are fairly evenly divided among the four profile types. One-quarter of them are directive, dominating individuals who love to take risks and make things happen. They thrive on problems and challenges, basking in productivity and making things happen around them. These people are the "doers" of society, people who set out to accomplish great things. For a church to appeal to them, they are likely to require challenging tasks, a viable means of connecting with a group of believers (since connecting is neither their natural tendency nor a strength) and a good sense of the benefits and parameters of the Christian life. They may chaff at or even resent a laidback ministry, since they are usually operating at full throttle. In fact, their aggressive approach to life and their failure to check the facts and build relationships before setting off to achieve something significant may rankle people – especially in the typically staid, predictable and high-control church world.

More than one-quarter of the unchurched are highly personable and energetic people. These are the classic extroverts who make life up as they go along and who motivate others through their upbeat personalities. Enthusiastic and entertaining, these folks love to be the center of attention and to get everyone involved in activities. They disdain control and details, and they work on raw energy and intuition.

About one-quarter of the unchurched fit the profile of those who are stabilizing forces, pursuing consistency, unity and continuity in their environment. These people are not pushy at all; compliance is one of their strengths. They strive for cooperation and serenity in their environment, and thrive on repetition and minimal change. These people are sometimes deemed "plodders" since they are reliable but slow-paced and resistant to innovation or creative ideas intruding on the known and the comfortable.

One out of every five unchurched adults is a cautious individual, driven to attend to the details and to be accurate. They rely on facts and work within parameters (e.g. laws, routines, instructions) and keep things orderly and on-track. They eschew risks and reserve judgment on issues until they have reliable information as the basis of their decisions. Their need for precision makes them seem overly critical; their need for planning and strategic thinking robs them of the joys that may emerge from spontaneity. They are suspect of quick decisions, do not trust others to do things right (and therefore do not delegate well) and are poor at finding compromises or diplomatic solutions.

TABLE 5.3
PERSONALITY FACTORS OF THE UNCHURCHED AND CHURCHED

	unchurched	churched
practical and sensible	90%	95%
logical and analytical	84	82
usually focused on the details	82	80
comfortable with big ideas	79	73
a real "people-person"	79	89
sensitive or highly emotional	62	56
highly creative	55	57
make decisions based on feelings	55	56
searching for meaning in life	45	42
not well-organized	31	28
shy or introverted	28	24

TABLE 5.4
PERSONAL STYLES OF THE UNCHURCHED

	un-churched	churched	Bible figures who exemplify this:
Dominance	25%	16%	Joshua, Paul, Solomon, Stephen
Interaction	27	32	Barnabas, Saul, Peter, David
Steadiness	21	25	Isaac, Abraham, Jonathan, Ruth
Cautiousness	20	21	Luke, Moses, Noah, Thomas

- "Dominance" – risk-taker, determined, decision-maker, competitive, problem-solver, productive, enjoys challenges, and goal-driven

- "Interaction" – energetic, very verbal, spontaneous, friendly, optimistic, thinks out loud, popular, motivates others

- "Steadiness" – loyal, avoids confrontation, dislikes change, patient, sympathetic, indecisive, sensitive, not demanding of others

- "Cautiousness" – accurate, practical, reserved, orderly, factual, likes instructions, detailed, conscientious

Note that unchurched adults are much more likely to be in the dominating group than are the churched. Unchurched adults are also somewhat less likely to be among the highly interactive, spontaneous people and are slightly less likely to be numbered among those who establish a steadying and stabilizing influence.

Does it make sense to you that the same type of church experience is going to satisfy the intellectual, emotional and spiritual needs of such diverse groups of people? Our past research has shown that churches do have a mixture of the four types within their congregations, but that the flavor or style of the church tends to attract a certain type of person more easily than it attracts others. Similarly, different types of people have greater impact with each of these groups than do others, and the church ministries to which a visitor is exposed may have varying degrees of appeal based upon their personal profile.

With just this information considered so far in this chapter you can see some of the challenges inherent in attracting, retaining and assisting the development of unchurched people. There are dozens of dynamics brewing beneath the surface that make penetrating their ranks so much more difficult than merely providing good music, comfortable seating and a stimulating sermon. For instance, there are also lifestyle issues...

INDICATORS RELATED TO LIFESTYLES

The overall pattern we have witnessed in our research is that the unchurched tend to be less engaged with the world than are churched adults. For example, they are more than 50% less likely to volunteer their time to help non-profit organizations; they are 17% less likely to engage in a discussion with friends on moral or ethical issues in a typical week; they are 14% less likely to be registered to vote; they are less likely to support non-profit organizations financially, and among the people who donate, the unchurched give to fewer organizations.

Politically, the unchurched are less likely to be registered as Republicans and more likely to be registered as Independents. Along the same lines, we found that they are twice as likely as the churched to describe themselves as "mostly liberal" on political and social issues, and only half as likely to say they are "mostly conservative" on such matters.

Technology has become a significant part of most people's lives. Our evaluation of the technology owned by the unchurched shows that they have a virtually identical ownership pattern to those of the churched. The only difference of merit was a slightly lower rate of ownership of cell phones, but the gap was not big enough to indicate a significant behavioral difference.

Interestingly, about one-third of the unchurched say that using the Internet has helped them to make and maintain friendships. Two-thirds of the unchurched who said this were under the age of 35. Also of importance was the finding that one-fifth of the unchurched adults noted that the Internet is a source of information they use regarding spirituality and matters of faith. Again, this tended to be a behavior of younger adults.

Even an examination of the types of non-profit organizations (NPOs) they have supported financially in the recent past shows that there are relatively few lifestyle differences in comparison to churched adults. The unchurched demonstrated a slightly lower inclination to give to each category of NPOs, with one exception: environmental groups. In that case, the unchurched were twice as likely to have given to organizations focused on defending the environment. Otherwise, they were slightly less likely to have donated to educational and youth agencies, to social welfare organizations, to medical and health care NPOs, to religious entities (other than churches), and to public service groups.

We also explored the perceptions of what types of organizations they feel are most worth supporting. Their attitudes in this regard tell us something about the qualities they deem to be most appealing – and, potentially, what they may be looking for in a church.

Surprisingly, their attitudes were hard to distinguish from those of the churched. Nine out of ten said they seek an organization that is known for integrity. Eight out of ten (78%) look for a compelling mission and vision that defines the activity of the organization – slightly less than the 86% of the churched who said this was very important, but generally similar in significance. Eight out of ten also said they evaluate the fiscal responsibility of an organization, and seven out of ten look for strong creative problem-solving skills. Only one-third said that having an ethnically diverse staff or leadership group makes a big difference to them. The least stock was placed in whether or not the leader of the organization is "articulate and charismatic;" only 12% said they deem that to be very important. That, too, is slightly lower than the importance assigned by the churched, but it remains the lowest rated item for both groups from among the six items tested.

LIFE PRIORITIES AND SATISFACTION

Some of the entryways into the lives of unchurched people become clearer once we examine their life priorities and how satisfied they are with the current state of their life in each of those areas. Table 5.5 presents information regarding the life outcomes that the unchurched deem to be most desirable in the future.

Right off the bat you'll probably notice that among the potential outcomes we tested, the response levels of the unchurched were significantly different from those of the churched on 17 of those 21 items! Most intriguing of all is the nature of the distinctions. The unchurched showed less enthusiasm than did the churched respondents in relation to 13 of those 17 items. Is it because they have set their sights lower? Is it because they are more realistic about what to expect? We cannot tell, but what we do know is that the life outcomes that were more compelling to the unchurched than to the churched related to leading "the good life." The unchurched were more desirous of having a comfortable lifestyle, a high-paying job, pleasure travel, and owning a large home. For achievement-oriented people with a spiritual vacuum in their life, these goals make sense.

49

TABLE 5.5
WHAT IS MOST DESIRABLE
FOR THEIR FUTURE
(% who said this is "very desirable" or their life in the future)

	Unchurched	Churched	Teens
having good physical health	85%	93%	87%
living with a high degree of integrity	73	85	71
having one marriage partner for life	70	85	82
having close, personal friendships	69	78	84
having a clear purpose for living	64	80	77
having a close relationship with God	44	84	66
having a satisfying sex life with your marriage partner	62	64	55
having a comfortable lifestyle	66	59	83
living close to your family and relatives	52	64	49
having children	48	58	54
being deeply committed to the Christian faith	20	70	50
being knowledgeable about current events	40	54	NA
making a difference in the world	37	52	56
being personally active in a church	11	57	43
having a college degree	38	42	88
influencing other people's lives	31	40	56
working in a high-paying job	36	26	55
traveling throughout the world for pleasure	31	24	NA
owning a large home	25	18	28
owning the latest household technology and electronic equipment	8	9	27
achieving fame or public recognition	8	5	18
sample size	327	675	605

Another significant revelation is that a majority of the churched prioritized the key faith outcomes tested, while only a minority of the unchurched did so. The churched are twice as likely to say they want a close relationship with God, and more than three times as likely to say they want to be deeply committed to the Christian faith. The churched are five times more likely to say they want to be active in a church, and they are about one-third more likely to express an interest in making a difference in the world. Clearly, as the unchurched chart their future, faith is not a major concern for most. We do not want to overlook the small core who do view faith development and connection as a priority – a group that constitutes perhaps a fifth of the segment – but in terms of the hierarchy of felt needs among most of the unchurched, faith development is MIA.

The other major takeaway from the data relates to the nature of what the unchurched are most focused upon for the future. There are seven items that a majority listed as priorities. Those items deal with health, relationships, purpose and character. The items that did not make the upper echelon of importance, besides faith, relate to family, service, and leisure.

In passing, also notice the responses of teenagers to future priorities. In relation to spiritual matters, they tend to lie somewhere between the unchurched and the churched. They are typically interested in having a close relationship with God (two-thirds desire that outcome), half are interested in being deeply committed to the Christian faith, and somewhat less than half of them would like to be active in a church. They tend to be very relational individuals – in fact, relationships are the driving force behind many of their choices and dreams in life – and therefore hope to have influence in people's lives and to make a difference in the world. But most teens are not sure that being connected with a church will enhance that opportunity. Do not lose sight of the fact that most teenagers are currently churched – they have a higher church participation rate than adults do! And yet they are not inclined to position organized religion at the hub of their future existence.

The life priorities described above gain greater context by examining the satisfaction levels detailed in Table 5.6. We asked a national sample of the unchurched to describe how satisfied they were with each of 15 dimensions of life. Using a six-point scale to convey their responses (ranging from extremely satisfied to not at all satisfied), the results are again enlightening. First, notice that a majority of the unchurched was either "extremely" or "very satisfied" in relation to only two of the 15 dimensions (i.e. their marriage and their personal character). However, there was not a single item among the list tested for which even seven out of every ten people was highly satisfied.

The value of the satisfaction ratings, however, is magnified by comparing those with the levels of importance assigned to each of the dimensions. For instance, we can see that only one out of every five unchurched adults is highly satisfied with their community involvement, but we also find that such efforts are a low priority to the unchurched, so there is not much likelihood that most unchurched people will do much about the low satisfaction they have in this regard. The same can be said for their satisfaction with their level of influence, their spiritual life, their current job and their educational achievement: their limited degree of satisfaction is mitigated by the comparatively low priority each of those items represents in their life.

The five dimensions that a majority of the unchurched defined as top priorities for their future were tested. We can see that while three-quarters said their personal character is important, only half of them feel that their character is measuring up to their own standards. Seven out of ten unchurched individuals said having a successful marriage is critical to them, but just two-thirds are highly satisfied with the condition of their marriage. Seven out of ten labeled friendships a top priority, but only half are highly satisfied with their current relationships. Two-thirds said that the quality of their life, overall, was a key consideration, yet barely two out of five say they are highly satisfied with that dimension of their life. Almost two-thirds claimed that having a satisfying sex life with their marriage partner was of top significance, but just half as many feel they are achieving that outcome. The biggest gap of all relates to personal health. More than four out of five unchurched adults said good health was a very desirable life product, but only one-third of them are extremely or very satisfied with the present state of their health.

In other words, if you can identify an area of life that an unchurched adult deems to be highly significant for his/her future, you can bet that they are at least moderately disenchanted with how they're doing in relation to that dimension. Whether or not they would be willing to take direction from a church to enhance their life in regard to that area of focus is another issue altogether.

TABLE 5.6
SATISFACTION LEVELS WITH
DIMENSIONS OF LIFE
(% who said they are "extremely" or "very" satisfied)

	unchurched	churched
your marriage*	65%	59%
personal character	52	51
family life	50	52
career choice*	48	49
friendships	47	51
overall lifestyle	42	41
current job*	40	44
educational achievement	39	38
spiritual life	35	45
sex life	34	36
health	32	38
leisure time	31	23
financial condition	29	25
level of influence	25	27
community involvement	19	22
sample size	287	746

(* indicates this was asked only among people to whom it was relevant)

We also asked the unchurched to describe to us the future possibilities that they consider to be most exciting. The specific items that topped the list included providing a good life for their children, experiencing technological breakthroughs, improved government performance and better physical health. Items related to career or financial success, when grouped together (described by about one-quarter of the group) emerged as the single, most alluring possibility. Only one out of every fifty unchurched people mentioned positive spiritual outcomes or progress as one of the potential outcomes that they found to be most exciting.

When we followed that up with a question about the future possibilities that troubled or worried them the most, the dominant concern was personal physical threats (war, street violence, physical crime). This issue outscored the second-most common concern (environmental decay) by a three to one margin. Again, this is an issue that relates closely to their concerns about quality of life and the ability to define themselves through their accomplishments.

So What?

So what does all of this information tell us about the unchurched?

Generally, these are individuals who do not see themselves as weak, needy or broken people. They are achievement-oriented, driven people who work with other human beings but are not as deeply concerned about people as the typical church person seems to be. As a group, they are quite matter-of-fact about life, and would probably have a hard time understanding notions like being "controlled by the Spirit" or "trusting God to direct your paths." They are self-reliant and have become comfortable with that approach to life.

Driven though they are, life is not producing the quality of experience that they desire. Most unchurched people could identify a half dozen or so areas of their life in which their experience is falling far short of their expectations. This undoubtedly contributes to their stress and frustration with life. Since many of these individuals are independent, self-reliant, problem-solving types of people, you can bet that they are constantly scanning the terrain for alternatives that might raise their fulfillment level a notch or two.

Although they have a spiritual side, they are not highly religious and few of them are seeking to increase their spiritual focus. If they do, their inclination would be to seek out groups that have a rather lenient, laissez faire theological approach, since their desire would be to retain control and authority over their life. They are also likely to search for churches that address the issues of greatest interest or concern to them – matters related to quality of life, means to achievement, and developing better relationships without having to become a highly relational person.

As you reach out to unchurched people, expect them to be generally ambivalent toward organized religion and even resistant to the ways of the church. Don't take it personally; their reaction is consistent with who they are and how they have coped with life to this point. Only a small percentage of the unchurched are actively seeking a deeper relationship with God, one that will allow Him to exert greater control over their life. They are not terribly interested in joining groups and their driven, independent nature makes them suspicious of people who suddenly strive to build friendships with them. They are not unreachable, but spiritual development is not on their "To Do" list. Influencing them with the things of God will take time, prayer and an intelligent strategy.

Six

THE
FAITH OF
THE UNCHURCHED

The issue is not whether or not the unchurched have faith. Every time they step on the brakes of their car they exhibit tremendous faith in gadgets that most of them know nothing about. Each time they go out in public, they are demonstrating faith in the behavior and morals of humankind, believing that they will not be shot or mugged. When they take a bite of food that has been prepared at a restaurant by a chef they never see or know, they are showing the faith they possess, believing that it was properly cooked and not that it was poisoned. Each time they deposit money in the bank, they are engaging in an act of faith, believing that their money will be returned to them, perhaps with interest. The issue is not whether or not they have faith, but in what do they place their faith?

As we will see, there is no easy answer to this question. Most unchurched people have some relationship with religion, spirituality and faith matters. However, the role and nature of faith looks and operates differently for them than for the two-thirds who are churched.

IN THE BEGINNING...

The cornerstone of Christian wisdom is the Bible. Our beliefs and life practices are to be in concert with those described for us in God's Word. More than nine out of ten churched people own multiple Bibles, and many of them even read it at least once a week.

Most of America's unchurched adults, in spite of their limited interest in organized religion, also own a Bible (75%). Two out of five of them believe that the Bible is either the literal Word of God or the inspired, inerrant Word. That's a much smaller slice of Bible believers than you find within the churched community (67%), but nevertheless it represents a sizeble foundation on which to build. In addition, one out of five unchurched adults contends that the Bible was inspired by God but contains historical and factual errors. The other one-third of the unchurched assert that the Bible is not God's Word at all, but is a book that was conceived and written by humans and is filled with errors and fallacies.

Whether they perceive it to be God's Word or not, awfully few of the unchurched read the Bible on a regular basis. Only 3% claim to read it daily. (For the sake of context, 17% of the churched say that they read the Bible every day.) In total, 15% read it at least once a week, 10% read it once a month, 12% at least once a quarter, 18% once or twice a year, and 21% on rare occasion. The remaining one-quarter never read the Bible.

One reason why so many unchurched adults may ignore the Bible is because of the version that they own. Without intending to denigrate the value of any particular version of the Bible, we know from extensive research on Bible usage that certain Bibles are easier than others for people to understand. The most difficult version to comprehend is the King James Version (KJV). In spite of that fact, the KJV remains the most widely used version in the country (although this is slowly changing as the avalanche of modern translations becomes better known and more widely trusted).

One of our recent surveys among the unchurched showed that while three-quarters of them own a KJV, a little less than half of them own another, more readable version. The low readership levels may be related to the fact that six out of ten unchurched people consider the KJV to be their primary reading version. No other version was named by even one out of ten unchurched adults. (In contrast, although three-quarters of the churched own KJVs, an even larger proportion owns a modern translation – although even among them ownership of the KJV outpaces its closest competitor by more than a 2 to 1 margin. Although the KJV is the most commonly used version among the churched, too, only one-third calls it their primary version.)

TABLE 6.1
BIBLE READING FREQUENCY

	unchurched	churched
weekly	15%	50%
monthly	10	14
quarterly	12	11
once/twice a year	18	7
less than once a year	21	4
never	25	8
sample size	273	727

WHAT DO THEY BELIEVE?

Indisputably, the unchurched are a study in contradictions when it comes to matters of faith. On the one hand, most unchurched people are not overly religious or spiritual, yet 70% call themselves Christian. Three-quarters of them own a Bible, but few read the contents. Almost half of them state that having a close, personal relationship with God is one of their top life priorities, but surprisingly few of them do much to facilitate that bond.

To get beyond the apparent inconsistencies and complexities and figure out how to minister to unchurched people, we have to understand their perception of the Christian faith. Many of them think of the Bible as an outdated book of rules, but a number of them believe it to be a relevant, useful guidebook to modern living. How they apply the perceived insights from Scripture depends on what they believe those insights to be. Let's examine the religious beliefs of the unchurched.

GENERAL BELIEFS

Two-thirds of the unchurched state that their religious faith is very important in their life today. Almost two-thirds of those individuals give strong (as opposed to moderate) affirmation to this notion. The older a person is, the more likely they are to possess this view. In fact, only one out of every four Baby Busters (i.e., adults 35 and under) concurred strongly with this view, compared to a majority of the 50-plus unchurched. The significance of faith was more strongly affirmed by political conservatives than by those who hold moderate and liberal views.

Consistent with their own low-key faith pursuits, most unchurched adults say that a person can lead a full and satisfying life even if they do not incorporate faith development into that life. Six out of ten unchurched adults accept this idea as accurate, while one-third rejects it. For most people, then, faith is an optional pursuit, a kind of bonus benefit that may prove to be useful.

BELIEFS RELATED TO DEITY

The more we explore the beliefs of the unchurched, the more contradictions we encounter. Seven out of ten unchurched adults believe that God originally created the universe. The nature of the God in which they believe, however, leaves much to be desired. Less than half of the unchurched (47%) believe that "God is the all-powerful, all-knowing, perfect creator of the universe who still rules the world today." (How can they explain this discrepancy? Did God create the world, watch for a while, then vanish? Did He create the universe but then lose His dominion over it?) Two out of ten say that "God" refers to a higher state of consciousness that people may achieve. One out of ten contend that God is the full realization of human potential. Six percent say everyone is God, the same number believe that there are many different gods, and 8% simply state that there is no such thing as God.

Beliefs about Jesus are no more consistent. Two-thirds contend that Jesus was born to a virgin. But His miraculous birthing fails to impress many of the unchurched. Half of them believe that Jesus sinned while He was on earth. Half also argue that He was crucified and died, but that He never had a physical resurrection. The sin nature of Jesus is attested to most heartily by people under 45 and by individuals who earn more than $75,000 annually.

They don't do much better with the Holy Spirit, either. Almost two-thirds of the unchurched deny the existence of the Third Person, saying that the Holy Spirit is a symbol of God's presence or power, but is not a living entity. (While we're on the topic, realize that the answers of the churched segment on this matter closely resemble those of the unchurched.)

BELIEFS ABOUT OTHER SPIRITUAL FORCES

Besides their bewilderment over the Trinity, people demonstrated tremendous confusion regarding one other spiritual power: Satan. Seven out of ten contended that Satan does not exist but is simply a symbol used to connote evil. (Once again, a parenthetical remark is in order: even a majority of the churched populace believes this lie.)

To their credit, most unchurched individuals (69%) do believe that angels exist and influence people's lives. Perhaps we should credit CBS, which brought us *Touched By An Angel*, for this widespread theological insight.

Isn't it interesting (and disheartening) that more people – be they churched or unchurched, believers or non-believers – accept the existence of angels than believe in the reality of the Holy Spirit or Satan?

BELIEFS ABOUT THE BIBLE

In a rare display of theological consistency, we found that 38% of the unchurched agree that the Bible is totally accurate in all that it teaches, which is nearly identical to the 39% who said that they perceive the Bible to be either the literal Word of God or His inspired Word without error. However, those individuals are divided among those who strongly agree that the Bible is completely accurate (22%) and those who are only somewhat convinced of that truth (16%). Of course, a majority (52%) does not buy into the idea at all, and another 10% don't know what to think.

There was a moderately strong relationship between socioeconomic status and agreement with the Bible's accuracy: the less education a person had completed, and the less income they earned, the more likely they were to accept the Bible as accurate. Stated differently, the more upscale a person was, the more skeptical they were about the Bible. There was also a substantial regional distinction in this regard. Unchurched Southerners were considerably more likely than unchurched adults from other regions to accept the accuracy of Scripture. Almost half of the unchurched people in the South (48%) accepted the Bible as accurate, compared to only one-third of all other unchurched (35%).

About half of the unchurched (55%) agreed that all of the miracles described in the Bible actually took place. Apparently, the difficulty that roughly one-sixth of the skeptics have with believing biblical content is not related to doubts about the miracles.

BELIEFS ABOUT SALVATION

The spiritual deception of the unchurched is perhaps most clear regarding salvation. In broad terms, we find that the unchurched generally reject the necessity of accepting Christ as savior, and instead believe that a person can earn his/her way into Heaven through good deeds, or even that there will not be any condemnation of anyone after death, no matter how they lived their life.

The contradiction here is that only one out of every four unchurched adults argues that sin is an outdated concept. Most of these folks accept the existence of sin, but do not believe that sin will have an eternal affect on an individual's ultimate destiny. Less than one out of five unchurched believe that there is no afterlife; and the remainder are divided between believing that everyone will experience the same, generally positive outcome, or that a person can earn eternal salvation through a preponderance of good deeds.

Amazingly, most of the unchurched believe that they will go to Heaven after they die, although few attribute that gift to the grace of God and their own profession of faith and acknowledgment of sin.

BELIEFS ABOUT OTHER FAITHS

Slightly more than half of the unchurched believe that all of the major faith groups in the world teach the same basic principles. An identical percentage of them (54%) believes that it does not matter what faith group you associate with because of the similarity in the principles being taught. This one-world-religion type of perspective is particularly prevalent among unchurched people under 40 years of age.

BELIEFS ABOUT PERSONAL RESPONSIBILITY

With regard to perceived responsibilities related to faith, there is some good news and some bad news. The bad news is that three-fourths of the unchurched believe that the Bible actually teaches that God helps those who help themselves. (The author of that line was actually Benjamin Franklin, whom few people have argued was one of God's inspired scribes.) This perspective is a natural fit among people who are admittedly self-sufficient and independent. This viewpoint is also a perfect summary of contemporary American theology: the world revolves around us, and God is welcome to piggyback on our efforts if He so desires. (Since this is the "bad news" paragraph, let me add one more disturbing tidbit: the response of churched people is identical on this issue to that of the unchurched.)

The good news is that relatively few of the unchurched (25%) believe that they have a responsibility to tell other people their religious beliefs. I am not rejecting evangelism – but I am thrilled that those who do not hold biblically accurate views have chosen to keep those views to themselves. The question that their opinion raises, of course, is whether they are silent about their beliefs simply because they are so uncertain about them or that those beliefs are not important to them, or because they believe that all people should keep their beliefs to themselves.

BELIEFS RELATED TO MORAL TRUTH

The question of whether or not absolute moral truth exists is a fundamental issue that determines the health or illness of our culture. Other research we have conducted throughout the past decade has emphasized our nation's movement toward the rejection of moral absolutes and the acceptance of moral relativism. Sadly, we have seen that born again Christians are nearly as likely as non-believers to reject moral absolutes, in spite of their professed allegiance to the Bible.

Given that, it should not be shocking to realize that the unchurched have gravitated toward relativism as their philosophy of choice. Only one out of every four unchurched adults believe that there is absolute moral truth that is knowable and unchanging. One-third believes that all truth is relative to the person and circumstances. Another three out of ten say that they have never thought about it—and, consequently, side with the "default" position of our culture, that of relativism. The remaining one-eighth simply has not arrived at a conclusion on the matter, although they, too, typically live in cooperation with the default position.

Moral truth is not the subject of regular reflection by the unchurched. Only one out of three say that they have spent any time at all thinking about the matter recently. In total, just one out of every four unchurched individuals characterize figuring out the existence of moral absolutes as very important. A larger (one-third) share says the matter is not important to them. A plurality (four out of ten) describes this issue as somewhat important.

These figures, in conjunction with other studies we have conducted, indicate that only a handful of unchurched adults operate with a biblical worldview as their decision-making filter in life.

TABLE 6.2
WHAT UNCHURCHED
AMERICANS BELIEVE
(N=1175)

statement	AST	ASW	DSW	DST
my religious faith is very important in my life	42%	24%	17%	14%
the Bible is totally accurate in all of its teachings	22	16	24	28
you, personally, have a responsibility to tell other people your religious beliefs	13	12	22	50
the devil, or Satan, is not a living being but is a symbol of evil	41	29	9	18
if a person is generally good, or does enough good things for others during their life, they will earn a place in Heaven	37	32	12	18
when He lived on earth, Jesus Christ was human and committed sins, like other people	22	26	10	28
it doesn't matter what religious faith you follow because they all teach the same lessons	27	27	16	26
the Holy Spirit is a symbol of God's presence or power but is not a living entity	35	28	9	16
after he was crucified and died, Jesus Christ did not return to life physically	29	18	12	25
the Bible teaches that God helps those who help themselves	50	26	5	10
all people will experience the same outcome after death, regardless of their religious beliefs	37	15	20	19

TABLE 6.2 (CONTINUED) WHAT UNCHURCHED AMERICANS BELIEVE

(N=1175)

statement	AST	ASW	DSW	DST
there are some crimes, sins or other things which people might do which cannot be forgiven by God	24	16	16	35
angels exist and influence people's lives	35	34	9	12
the universe was originally created by God	53	18	9	12
the whole idea of sin is outdated	12	11	19	52
you can lead a full and satisfying life even if you do not include spiritual development in your life	35	24	14	21
people who do not consciously accept Jesus Christ as their savior will be condemned to Hell after they die	15	8	18	54
Jesus Christ was born to a virgin	47	18	9	14
all of the miracles described in the Bible actually happened	38	17	16	20
all of the major religious groups of the world teach the same principles.	27	27	16	26

KEY: AST = agree strongly; ASW = agree somewhat; DSW = disagree somewhat; DST = disagree strongly.

NOTE: Percentages may not add to 100% because the "don't know" response is not included in this table.

LEVEL OF COMMITMENT

Not surprisingly, among the 70% who label themselves "Christian," the commitment level is not very high. Overall, just 11% say that they are absolutely committed to Christianity and another 29% say they are moderately committed. Most of the unchurched are even less committed: 15% say not too, and 44% say not at all committed.

If we project the statistics to the entire segment of the unchurched, and add a couple of other facts from our research, we arrive at the following profile:

- 14% are atheists

- 16% align themselves with other faith groups

- 8% call themselves Christian and say they are "absolutely committed"

- 20% call themselves Christian and say they are "moderately committed"

- 11% call themselves Christian and say they are "not too committed"

- 31% call themselves Christian and say they are "not at all committed"

Certainly one of the warnings to us inherent in these numbers is that when a person describes himself as a Christian, we cannot take his statement at face value. Because the term "Christian" has become so generic in our culture, we need to probe a bit to discover what type of "Christian" the individual is – ranging from the nominal, in-name-only Christian to a deeply devout follower of Jesus. There are many shades of alleged Christianity in-between those end points. Accepting someone's personal description might be more harmful than helpful to them and to the Church.

Notice that only one out of every seven unchurched adults is an atheist. Naturally, those individuals will require an entirely different strategy if we are to get them to connect with the Church. Knowing that six out of seven people at least have some self-perception of a religious connection paves the way for constructive and fruitful outreach built on a foundation of basic belief in God.

Keep in mind that 15% of the unchurched adults in our country say they will "definitely" return to church within the next three months, and another one-quarter (23%) say they "probably" will return. This is a return to levels we measured in 1986, and substantially higher than the levels measured in 1990 and 1995. Millions of unchurched adults are open to the possibility of re-attaching to a faith community.

Our experience in researching people's projected future behavior tells us that the "likely to return" estimates are overly optimistic. A more realistic assessment of the number of adults who might return to a church is in the 13% to 16% range. The experience those individuals have at the church they visit may well determine whether they stay connected or leave again – perhaps for good.

BORN AGAIN, BORED AGAIN

We also discovered that almost one out of five unchurched adults – 18% – is a born again Christian. By that term we mean that they say they have made a personal commitment to Jesus Christ that is still important in their life today, and that they know they will go to Heaven when they die because they have confessed their sins and accepted Jesus Christ as their savior.

(We do not ask people to designate themselves as "born again." We categorize them as such according to how they answer the two items just described regarding salvation.)

There are some pretty significant implications to the fact that one-fifth of the unchurched are born again. One of the considerations relates to church dropouts and retention. The fact that such a substantial slice of the adult born again population – about 15% of the total – could walk away from the church without any intention of returning ought to make us pause and reflect on how we can more effectively retain believers within the church. It's one thing for people to accept a credit card and return it, join a health club and drop their membership, or register to vote then fail to show up on election days, but here we're talking about an eternal relationship with God Himself, and maintaining it in the company of other believers. What can we learn from the dropouts to prevent future defections from the church, not to salvage the institution, but for the sake of their spiritual health and for the good of the kingdom?

A second consideration concerns the prospects for church growth. If just the born again adults who are unchurched returned to the church, that would represent an influx of more than 12 million adults (along with perhaps another 4 to 6 million kids). To give you some idea of just how many people that represents, if we were to distribute those 12 million adults evenly among the 324,000 Protestant churches in America, the increase would amount to 37 adults per church. Given that the average church is only 90 adults, this growth would constitute more than a 40% expansion of the typical church. (Naturally, these assumptions are for illustrative purposes; if the scenario described were to occur, it would stand as one of God's most amazing miracles.) Guiding those 12 million people back to the church would go down in the history books as one of the great revivals of all time.

Okay, back to reality. Even if all 12 million unchurched believers do not return to the church within the next few years, a significant proportion of them could be attracted back. We found that the dominant reasons for their avoidance of the church are lack of time and lack of interest: these two reasons cover about three out of five of the unchurched believers. Very few of these people stay away because of bad past experiences (less than 5%); more often, they duck the church because of irrelevant past experiences. Providing them with a high-value experience – genuine worship, relevant discipleship, sincere and caring relationships, meaningful opportunities for gift-based service, loving accountability, an environment ripe for productive evangelism – would ring the bells of millions of these wayward family members. Convincing them that they could have such an experience would be perhaps the toughest challenge in the process; but if we deliver the goods, they are likely to re-enlist.

SPIRITUAL INVOLVEMENT AND EXPOSURE

Having just railed against the superficial faith commitment of the unchurched, let me now show that few of them have completely insulated themselves from religious exposure.

The defining characteristic of the unchurched, of course, is that they do not attend church services. However, they voluntarily gain exposure to a host of other religious and spiritual influences. Here is a list of some of those experiences.

- Half of the unchurched pray to God in a typical week.
- Three out of ten have a quiet time or devotional time during an average week.
- One out of every seven reads from the Bible during the week; one out of four does so in a typical month. Roughly the same number read from a book of sacred literature other than the Bible in an average month.
- One out of every ten is engaged in a spiritual mentoring process.

- Very few engage in group activities such as Sunday school classes (2% attend in a typical week) or a small group (3%).
- One out of every ten purchased Christian music in the preceding year.
- Three out of ten watch religious television programming in a typical month.
- One out of four listen to Christian radio programming during an average month.
- One out of five read a Christian magazine during an average 30-day period.

When you put it all together, you discover that slightly more than three-quarters of the unchurched have some type of self-initiated interaction with religious activity or information. There is a reasonable chance of reaching these individuals with a positive, church-building message – if we are strategic about the process.

THE LIKELIHOOD OF RETURNING TO A CHRISTIAN CHURCH IN THE NEAR FUTURE

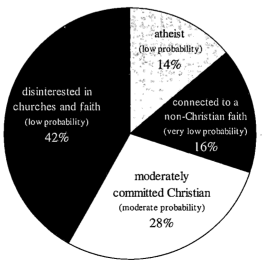

So What?

There are significant opportunities to penetrate the unchurched market with God's love and truth. While there is a hardcore segment that is not ready to be reached yet, there are millions of people disconnected from the church who are ripe for reconnection. One out of every seven are likely to visit a church in the coming three to six months, seeking a spiritual home. Twice as many (one-third of the unchurched) admit that they are more likely to be looking for spiritual answers to address the problems and challenges they face in life than they were to turn to faith solutions three years ago. The unchurched are not going to come to us, but if we initiate appropriate contact and deliver on our promises and fulfill their spiritual needs, millions of unchurched people can be aligned with a Christian church.

To make the most of the opportunities that exist, and to create additional opportunities, recognize that the unchurched market is divided into self-defined niches. The people within each of those niches have different degrees of likelihood of joining the Church. Overall, 16% are associated with other, non-Christian religions (lowest probability of aligning with a local church); 14% are atheists (a low probability of joining us); 28% think of themselves as committed Christians (highest probability of reconnecting); and 42% are neither interested in organized religion nor consider faith to be a major life issue (low probability of returning to a church).

What can you do to increase the interest of the unchurched in returning to the fold? Here are some possibilities.

- Give an unchurched friend a copy of a modern translation of the Bible. The New King James, the New International, the Living Translation and other recent entries into the Bible market might help God's Word to come alive for these individuals. Such a gift must be handled deftly or else it may seem too pushy or even arrogant. If you have the chance to discuss life issues together, and you identify key issues on which you have differing opinions, you might "tease" them into examining their Bible by explaining how you arrived at your stand on the issue through the application of Bible content, and offering to give them a user friendly version.

- Take Peter's exhortation seriously: always be prepared to give a reason for the hope that is within you (1 Peter 3:15). Most Americans, even the unchurched, are seeking hope. Think through how you could sensitively but persuasively (not offensively or aggressively) communicate the reasons for your faith in practical, non-religious terminology.

- Grace is a concept that millions of Americans don't understand. Yet, it is a cornerstone concept for people to comprehend if they are going to accept God's grace offered to us through the death and resurrection of Jesus. Reflect on pragmatic ways of describing what both the concept and the experience of that grace has meant to you.

- Learn to listen for the underlying foundations of people's arguments. Often you will discover that their fundamental assumptions include the rejection of absolute moral truth. Without becoming argumentative or philosophically obtuse, develop the skill of identifying the fallacy of people's truth assumptions, and how to inoffensively propose an alternative for their consideration. Paul was a great role model in this regard, seeking to understand the cultural assumptions of his audience, then discussing a divergent but reasonable point of view in ways that made him interesting. (See Acts 17 for a revealing illustration of this principle in action.)

- Before inviting your unchurched associates to a church, take the time to examine it through their eyes. Is your church accessible and comprehensible to someone who is not a believer, or to a person who has little knowledge of the Bible, or to one who is unfamiliar with how the church works? Our studies have found that sometimes we have done more harm by inviting unchurched people to a particular church – i.e. one that was unsuited to their needs or unprepared to reach out to them – than would have been done by enveloping them in a web of faith-based relationships or exposing them to carefully-chosen spiritual experiences other than worship services or regular church programs. There is a church that is right for everyone, but it may not be yours. If you discover, after assessing your church through their eyes, that it is not really unchurched-friendly, take the initiative to do something about it.

Seven

WHAT THE UNCHURCHED WANT FROM A CHURCH

Family counselors will tell you that one of the greatest destroyers of marriages is the failure of spouses to communicate with each other. Conflict and disappointment are inevitable results in any relationship, but the key is not to eliminate their occurrence as much as how to address those challenges. Understanding the nature and emergence of those elements are crucial factors in developing appropriate and timely solutions.

The same principle holds true in reaching and ministering to the unchurched. We cannot hope to be effective in our efforts to guide them to the cross and integrate them to a community of faith if we do not comprehend the issues that they have with the Church and the personal needs and expectations they possess regarding spirituality and church life. In this chapter, let's examine our research concerning what unchurched people want from a church.

THE ENTRY POINT

One of the disturbing revelations that emerged from our research is that most pastors, and a large share of Christian individuals, have restricted their thinking about reaching the unchurched down to attracting them to a worship service. Given that the fundamentals of authentic Christian living encompass worship, discipleship, stewardship, evangelism, service, and relationships with other believers, the significance of worship services is not to be dismissed. However, pushing to get unchurched people reconnected with God and His Church solely by means of a worship service is shortsighted.

If we examine the attitudes of the unchurched, we discover that a majority of them indicate that the best way to get them connected to a Christian church is *not* through a worship service. Those events were, by far, the most common answer offered as to how to enter the faith community, but only four out of ten unchurched adults said that worship services would be their preferred means of access. One out of five said they would prefer to connect through special events that were open to all people, both regulars and outsiders. One out of seven expressed an interest in participating in community service activities. Less than one out of ten listed each of various other options, including small classes held specifically for visitors, small groups, and Sunday school classes.

The youngest adults expressed the least interest in worship services. Their preferences revealed an interest in more relational experiences, such as community outreach projects or special events that connected people from outside and inside the church. Worship services had their greatest appeal among blacks, residents of the Midwest and individuals who possessed the "Cautious" behavioral type (see chapter 5).

TABLE 7.1
THE DESIRED ENTRY POINT TO
ATTRACT THE UNCHURCHED

worship service	40%
special event open to all people	19
community outreach activity	15
small class for church visitors	6
small group at someone's home	5
adult Sunday school class	4
not sure; depends on situation	11

The point to take away from these statistics is not that it is bad to invite unchurched people to worship services, or that they won't attend them. The data suggest that a large proportion of the unchurched would expect to reconnect with a church through that very means. The key revelation is that there must be multiple routes of entry available to unchurched people. Just as some people get back into physical exercise through different means – aerobics, jogging, swimming, machines that promote heart exertion, racquetball, team sports, and so forth – so will Americans choose to return to church through various approaches. We cannot afford to put all of our eggs in the "worship basket" if we're serious about reaching as many as we can for the kingdom of God.

IT'S ALL ABOUT PEOPLE

One perspective became very clear through our two-year study of the unchurched: their likelihood of returning to and remaining at a church largely depends upon the nature of the people who go there. Theology matters, but in the minds of the unchurched (and, quite frankly, most of the churched), the friendly and caring nature of the people matters more. One veteran of the church who had dropped out and was considering a return described it this way: "I probably wouldn't know good religious teaching from bad, or a great sermon from one that breaks every rule in the preaching manual. But I sure know nice people from jerks, and real people from hypocrites. I'd stay at a church with lousy teaching but genuinely friendly people, people who got to know me and cared about me and respected my needs and boundaries, before I'd stay at a place with perfect teaching and lousy people."

About two-thirds of the unchurched told us that when they recalled the things they liked about the churches they had visited in the past, what they remember most vividly were the people. They felt drawn to the community and to the authentic faith struggles of the people in those places. They may not have understood or embraced the same values as all of the church regulars, but they respected the honest effort being made to clarify and incorporate those values. Slightly more than one-third of the unchurched recalled with warmth the preaching and teaching at the churches they had attended, but the intellectual or substantive emphasis was less meaningful than the emotional or relational emphasis of churches for most people. The environment of the church – how formal or casual, how inviting or uninviting, how physically comfortable or uncomfortable, how uplifting or negative the atmosphere – was fondly remembered by one out of every five of the unchurched. Almost as many cited different elements of the church's corporate ministry, such as the music or traditions. Only a few (5%) listed programs or ministry activities of the church.

The significance of the personal touch at church is especially intriguing in light of our finding that unchurched people are not as relational as the typical churched individual. The focus on relational connections also raises the question of why unchurched individuals left the church they were attending if they felt so cared for and connected. The answer turns out to be that the unchurched were not sufficiently tied into the lives of the church people to feel completely connected. Combined with the other pressures they were facing in their lives, the limited importance they attached to preaching and Bible teaching, and their ambivalence toward worship, they did not feel compelled to continue to be part of a church.

THE LOST, AND VARIATIONS THEREOF

One of the most enlightening insights from our research concerns the language that we use to describe unchurched people, especially those who do not know Christ as their savior. Our observation of churches across the country is that one of the most common terms used is "the lost." Undoubtedly you have heard many of the popular expressions in the church world these days. "Lost people matter to God." "Our goal is to reach the lost at any cost." "We must bring the lost into a right relationship with God." "Bring your lost friends to church." "Until you build bridges to the lost people in our community, there is no clear pathway for them to follow on the route to spiritual wholeness."

Put yourself in the shoes of a person who is not connected to Jesus. Assume that you are somewhat interested in discovering more about the possibilities of developing a deeper relationship with Him, and that you might even be willing to associate with a church that could facilitate your spiritual growth. After checking around, you identify a church that might be a good place to start your explorations. To your satisfaction, you hear them describe your situation. To your horror, you hear them label you "lost." In your mind, that is a demeaning, arrogant and inaccurate term. It is also a very revealing term regarding the heart of the people who use the word: they cannot be loving, understanding people if they would elevate themselves to a place of knowing what is right while anyone who believes differently is inferior or "lost."

Does that sound far-fetched? It's not. In fact, it describes a fairly common scenario in which the unchurched misinterpet what we mean and depart from the church emotionally bruised. In our surveys we found that 56% of the unchurched said that they find the term offensive; only 6% said they would look favorably upon a church that described them in that way.

So, what do they want to be called? We tested seven terms. The two most acceptable terms were "inquirer" and "explorer," each of which was embraced by about half of the unchurched. Even the widely-used term "seeker" was not as popular; only four out of ten said they preferred that term. Expressions that get into the "offensive" territory included "non-Christian," "prodigal," "lost," and non-believer." The terms "non-Christian" and "non-believer" were rejected because most of these people deem themselves to be Christian; their rejection of the church and their not having a real or growing relationship with Jesus Christ were seen as irrelevant to the issue.

TABLE 7.2
WHAT DO THE UNCHURCHED
WANT TO BE CALLED?

preferred term	like it	subgroups especially fond of this label
inquirer	52%	men; parents; Democrats
explorer	48	men
seeker	40	Midwesterners
non-Christian	20	liberals; never-been-married
prodigal	13	born again Christians; blacks
lost	11	---
non-believer	10	college graduates

Don't overlook the tone of the two terms that were the most popular. "Inquirer" and "explorer" are words that suggest they are still in the hunt, that they have not given up on faith or spiritual development, even though they may have given up on the local church. The low standing of "non-believer" is consistent with this drive to remain a player in the spiritual realm.

TREATING THEM RIGHT

The unchurched have some very definite feelings about what they do and do not want to experience if they return to a church. The information in Table 7.3 describes what they like and dislike. These attitudes can help us to craft an intelligent and strategic approach to helping their exposure to your church be the most positive adventure possible.

As you examine the data, you will see that the most popular reactions to their presence at the church are very low-key responses. Three out of four would like to get a note in the mail from the pastor acknowledging their presence and thanking them for coming. Three out of four would like to be given information about the church that they could read in their own place, on their own time. Three out of four said they would like the church to do nothing special or unusual for them while they are visiting; they'd like to simply know what it's like to be at the church, without anyone creating an artificial response to their presence.

Three out of five said they wouldn't mind if a church had a special reception for visitors – after the service – to welcome and get to know them. (We have learned that they want this to be after the service so that they can figure out whether or not it is a reception worth going to, that is, if they would consider returning to the church.) Three out of five were willing to field a telephone call from either the pastor or someone from the church – interestingly, it really doesn't make much difference to them – during the week after their visit, to thank them for attending and to answer any questions they might have.

TABLE 7.3
HOW THE UNCHURCHED WANT TO BE TREATED AT CHURCH

Like this response?	Yes	No	Not sure
received a thank you note from the pastor during the week after the visit, thanking you for visiting and inviting you to return	78%	13%	10%
they gave you information about the church	72	16	8
they did not do anything special for you or treat you any differently than anyone else	76	17	7
members of the church came to you after the service and individually greeted you because you were visiting	72	22	7
they held a reception after the church service for church members to welcome and get to know visitors	64	28	8
you received a telephone call from the pastor to thank you for visiting and to ask if you have any questions about the church	61	29	9
you received a telephone call from someone from the church, other than the pastor, to thank you for visiting and to ask if you have any questions about the church	61	32	7

TABLE 7.3 (CONTINUED)
HOW THE UNCHURCHED WANT TO BE
TREATED AT CHURCH

Like this response?	Yes	No	Not sure
during the offering or collection they mentioned that they did not expect visitors to give money, since that is the responsibility of the people who are members of the church	46%	32%	23%
someone from the church, other than the pastor, visited your home during the week after your visit to drop off a small gift, such as plate of cookies or loaf of bread, to thank you for visiting their church	45	47	8
they offered you a free audio tape of the church service that you could get after the service	41	47	12
they asked you to identify yourself during your visit, so that people would know you were a visitor	39	55	6
they asked you to wear a special visitor's name tag	35	57	8
the pastor visited your home during the week after your visit to the church	34	58	8
someone from the church, other than the pastor, visited your home during the week after your visit to the church	30	62	8

After that, interest drops considerably. Less than half of the unchurched expressed interest in any of the remaining responses. Those included knowing that they are not expected to donate during their visit; receiving a small gift at their home for having attended; identifying themselves as a visitor during their visit; wearing a special visitor's name tag; or being visited at home, by either the pastor or someone else from the church. Our interviews indicate that control is a major issue. The unchurched do not want people exerting control over them. In this regard, the gift brought to their home may seem like manipulation. Identifying themselves makes them a target of unnatural attention. The home visit is an invasion of their turf and ignores their busy schedule. (To be clear about this, these people resist home visits that are *unrequested*; if they have invited you to their home, that is a different story.)

Different segments of the unchurched responded more favorably than did others to certain types of treatment. Adults under 35, for instance, resonated with mentioning that visitors are not expected to provide a financial gift during the offertory. The least educated people expressed the greatest interest in getting a telephone call from someone, getting a gift, and being visited by the pastor. Adults with the highest levels of education were less interested than were other people in wearing nametags, having a gift dropped off, or receiving a gift delivered to their home by a church member. Residents of the West were much less interested than other people in wearing nametags and going to receptions after the service. Although most of the unchurched people in the South agreed that they did not want anything special to be done for them, they were less likely to say this than were people living elsewhere. Southerners, and especially black adults, were interested in a visit from the pastor.

Since we started tracking the movement of the unchurched fifteen years ago, we have seen some very significant shifts in how they want to be treated by churches. Table 7.4 displays some of the transitions pertinent to the past decade. Notice that there is less timidity among the unchurched these days about being identified during their visit or about being contacted afterwards. This is attributable to two changes: the growing sense of disconnection and loneliness in America, and the relational emphasis of the Baby Busters and Mosaics. Things have not gotten to the point where it is an "anything goes," open invitation to communicate at will with them, but there is a definite loosening up of the restrictions they feel about making contact with them.

TABLE 7.4
HOW DESIRED TREATMENT OF THE
UNCHURCHED HAS CHANGED IN THE
PAST DECADE

	Like this response		
	2000	1995	1990
received a thank you note from the pastor during the week after the visit, thanking you for visiting and inviting you to return	78%	70%	70%
they gave you information about the church	72	70	74
they did not do anything special for you or treat you any differently than anyone else	76	79	56
members of the church came to you after the service and individually greeted you because you were visiting	72	78	67
they held a reception after the church service for church members to welcome and get to know visitors	64	65	60

TABLE 7.4 (CONTINUED)
HOW DESIRED TREATMENT OF THE
UNCHURCHED HAS CHANGED IN THE
PAST DECADE

	2000	1995	1990
you received a telephone call from the pastor or someone else from the church to thank you for visiting and to ask if you have any questions about the church	61%	60%	63%
someone from the church, other than the pastor, visited your home during the week after your visit to drop off a small gift, such as plate of cookies or loaf of bread, to thank you for visiting their church	45	22	NA
they asked you to identify yourself during your visit, so that people would know you were a visitor	39	22	23
they asked you to wear a special visitor's name tag	35	26	21
the pastor visited your home during the week after your visit to the church	34	33	34

MINISTRY EMPHASIS

The research also reminds us that different people are turned on by different elements of ministry. We asked the unchurched what type of church they would prefer, based upon the ministry emphasis of the church. Their answers were divided rather evenly among the four choices we provided. One-quarter would prefer a church whose emphasis was upon serving the needy people in their area. One-quarter would prefer a church with an evangelistic emphasis. One-fifth was most interested in a church that stresses teaching the Bible. One-sixth was seeking a place whose dominant emphasis was on building relationships, support and accountability among believers. The remaining one out of eight people did not have any idea what type of church they would want – but a large share of those people are individuals who have a very limited likelihood of returning to the church (i.e. atheists and people with no interest in faith).

The matter of ministry emphasis did define specialized niches within the unchurched community, though. A majority of the born again adults expressed an interest in an evangelistic congregation. A highly relational ministry was of comparatively greater interest to people living in the Northeast. A church focused on serving the needy was attractive to the most affluent of the unchurched, to people who are politically and socially liberal, and to residents of the West.

THE IDEAL CHURCH

To once again demonstrate the diversity of preferences among the unchurched, we asked them to make choices between eleven pairs of possibilities pertaining to what type of church they would ideally like to attend. There was only one factor for which even half of the unchurched indicated that they had a strong preference – and that was only 52% who said they would prefer attending a church of 200 people to a church of 1000. There are almost as many combinations of preferences as there are unchurched people.

We did find, however, that there are a number of leanings that the unchurched possess. For instance, if the majority (or plurality) were to rule, churches would provide traditional music

TABLE 7.5
THE PREFERRED ELEMENTS
OF A CHURCH

options	prefer this option:		
	strongly	somewhat	total
A: service with traditional hymns or	26%	21%	47%
B: service with contemporary worship music	14	16	30
A: with a formal worship service	18	18	36
B: with an informal worship service	23	26	48
A: with less than 100 people attending	30	26	55
B: with more than 300 people attending	8	14	22
A: with less than 200 people attending	52	24	77
B: with more than 1000 people attending	3	3	7
A: service that has everyone participate throughout the service	33	20	53
B: service with little participation, where the people watch the leaders conduct the service	17	17	34
A: service where children attend with their parents, and there is a section of the service geared to children	43	13	56
B: service just for adults, with children enrolled in classes that meet else-where during the adult service	23	10	33
A: with a choir that is accompanied by an organ	29	24	53
B: with a singer who leads the congregation in songs, accompanied by a band playing electric instruments	12	11	23

TABLE 7.5 (CONTINUED)
THE PREFERRED ELEMENTS
OF A CHURCH

options	prefer this option: strongly	somewhat	total
A: where people raise their hands, applaud and make other verbal affirmations or noises during the musical portion of the worship service	18%	13%	31%
B: where people are reserved and orderly during the service	35	21	55
A: where communion is offered as part of service	26	18	44
B: where communion is offered only at special services at other times of the year	17	17	34
A: where time is set aside for people to pray with or minister to each other during the service	29	21	51
B: where there is no interaction among people during the service, other than a brief greeting to those seated nearby	17	20	37
A: where the sermons address issues or concerns that people face in their lives	44	19	62
B: where the sermons are based on studying a specific book of the Bible, with a verse by verse explanation of those	15	6	21

(including a choir and organ), topical sermons, an informal environment, congregations of less than 200 people, substantial participation in the service by everyone, children attending the service with their parents, a reserved and orderly service, and time set aside within the service for people to pray for and minister to each other.

Upon exploring various niches, though, divergent combinations of preferences were expressed. Each of these groups would create churches and church services that look and feel quite different. Here are a few examples of those combinations.

- People under 35 would prefer a service that includes music – both traditional and contemporary – played by an electric band with a "worship leader." They want kids to attend the service with their parents (perhaps because they feel they never received the nurture they wanted), and they'd prefer a service with more than 300 people. Their ideal service would facilitate a lot of congregational participation and allow time for people in the congregation to minister to each other during the service.

- People 50 and older would prefer a service that features traditional hymns and that unfolds in an orderly and reserved manner – no raising of hands, applauding and making noise during the service, and no children accompanying their parents to the service. These older individuals do not want time set aside for interaction among congregants, other than the turn-and-greet routine, during the service. They also prefer services that require a minimum of participation by those in the sanctuary.

- Black adults would opt for services in which the entire family attends together, there is a high level of personal involvement in the service, and there is a high degree of expressiveness – clapping, shouting, applauding, and the like. They would prefer services in which time is included for people to pray with and minister to each other during the service, as well as time set aside for communion during each service.

- Whites, on the other hand, lean toward an informal service, but one that is more orderly and reserved.

- Adults in the South would create an informal atmosphere for congregations of 200 or fewer people. They would use contemporary worship music provided by an electric band with a music leader out front and seek substantial participation in the service by everyone present. Communion would be reserved for special services and events held throughout the year, but time would be included in each week's service for attenders to pray with and minister to each other.

- People in the upper income ranges also vied for an informal atmosphere and for contemporary worship music. However, they also wanted a service that required limited participation from people, reserved and orderly behavior, children shuffled off to classes, and no time set aside to pray for and minister to others during the service. They, like most people, would like to be in a congregation of less than 200 people.

Among the more surprising outcomes from this exercise are that such a large proportion of the unchurched feel more comfortable with traditional church music than with contemporary worship music, including a preference for choirs and organs rather than guitars and drums; the desire to have time within the service for interpersonal ministry; and their preference for churches of 200 or fewer people. How does this fit?

Traditional church music not only appeals to most of the people 50 and older, but it also appeals to a stunning percentage of people under 35. One of the hallmarks of that group, of course, is their need for moorings in life and, within the church context, that often means returning to music and traditions that give them greater cohesion and foundations in life. (The unique twist among the young adults, though, is that they would prefer the old-time hymns be played by an electric band, with a "worship leader" out front, and a contemporary feel to those hymns.)

The desire for time to minister to each other is a reflection of the national trends toward greater participation in every event experienced, people's desire for control over their environment, the drive toward increased lay ministry, and the expanding sense of alienation and loneliness. Many people look at their church experience as an opportunity to address their need to take responsibility for the shaping and development of their life, including how they are ministered to and their own ability to be a spiritual helper to others.

The preference for smaller churches rather than megachurches is also surprising. Especially in light of their desire to remain somewhat anonymous during their initial visits to a church, you might have anticipated the unchurched to automatically gravitate to larger congregations. However, they chose smaller churches. A major reason goes back to their desire for personal connections. Their assumption is that they will have an easier time of connecting with people, of gaining some level of significance, and of finding a more welcoming atmosphere in a small church.

Why, then, do so many of the unchurched wind up returning to a megachurch? Because the people in those large churches are more likely to invite outsiders to visit than are the people who attend smaller churches. Many small churches are so small because their people are comfortable being small; each time a newcomer visits, the security of the known is dissipated a bit, creating greater discomfort for them. In contrast, one of the common expectations expressed to the people who attend larger churches is that they should invite their unchurched friends.

Large churches, in other words, become large because they strive to become large; small churches remain small because they typically possess a small-church mentality. Thus, even though most unchurched people might prefer a small church, many of them wind up at a large church. The catalyst behind the leanings of a church – that is, whether to remain small or go for size – is leadership. Large churches embrace the attitude of growth because the church leadership promotes that mindset. In smaller churches, leadership often focuses on internal ministry rather than external outreach.

So What?

The information regarding what people want from a church once again emphasizes that there are many different tastes, needs and expectations among the unchurched. Your church might be just what God intends it to be, yet it may not be at all attractive to certain unchurched people–and that is to be expected, given the "satisfy me with a customized experience" mind set of growing numbers of Americans.

Ultimately, the key to the process turns out to be the people in the church. Outsiders visit a church looking for insiders who are sensitive to the unchurched person's background and needs; who will be flexible enough to adjust to some of those needs; and whose demeanor and behavior are a stellar example of authentic Christianity in action. It used to be that unchurched people complained that churches spent too much time and effort raising money from congregants. That is no longer the issue du jour. The new point of irritation is the alleged hypocrisy of the congregants.

In practical terms, then, a church would be better off ensuring that its people are living a Christian life to the fullest – full joy, complete consistency of church teaching and personal lifestyles, openness to enfolding newcomers into their family of faith – than to launch marketing efforts, program changes and special events designed to attract unchurched people. Events, programs and advertising might attract a person to visit once, but unless they sense that the church is a place of internal consistency and overt love, they won't come back – either to your church or, often, to any other.

Think of it this way: your responsibility is bigger than whether or not you grow numerically. Each time an unchurched individual visits your church and chooses not to return, their experience with you may well determine their likelihood of ever returning to a Christian church. You cannot force an individual to stay, nor can you guarantee that your church will satisfy all of their needs. You can ensure , however, that they leave knowing that your church was a dynamic and positive expression of what Jesus must have had in mind when He said that the gates of Hades would not overcome His Church (Matt. 16:18).

Eight

GETTING THEIR ATTENTION

With the onslaught of technology in recent years, the number of methods that are available to us through which we can convey tailored messages to the unchurched has grown considerably. Of course, not every method is amenable to the church's mission and values, some methods are not cost-effective and not every message is compelling and appropriate.

Your decision about the ways in which you will reach out to unchurched people will have a tremendous impact upon your ability to minister successfully to the group. The message you choose to convey will position you in their minds in either a positive, negative or indifferent way. The media that you use to communicate with them will either give your message the audience it needs or simply drain your church's limited resources. These choices matter, just as your decision of how to minister to the unchurched once they visit your church or engage with your people is of vital importance.

Let me emphasize the significance of remaining competitive in the marketplace. These are not the good ol' days when people were meaningfully connected to a network of other people in their neighborhood and at work. This is not the era when people knew the names of the churches in their community, and probably knew which people in the neighborhood attended what church. No longer do people look to churches to provide guidance on key moral and local issues. Churches, with amazing swiftness, are becoming the invisible institutions of our communities.

In a recent national survey among the unchurched, we found that only half of them (51%) claimed that they could remember the name of even one church within a fifteen-minute drive from their house. (By the way, we have also discovered that when people say they can recall such information, the chances are good that many of them cannot actually do so, which makes the statistic above an overestimate of reality.) We also know that many of the people who say they can name a local church identify places by generic names; "First Baptist," "the Lutheran Church," "the Catholic Church," and "First Methodist" are some common examples of the vague names that get listed. Our studies also show that in many communities around the country, when we have the ability to check the church names that are provided to us against the names of existing churches in that area, fewer than one out of four unchurched adults can name at least one existing church nearby.

In fact, we discovered that only two out of every three unchurched people (65%) even know someone who attends a church in the area. This is a serious decline from the days when even if you did not attend church, you knew many people who did. The implication is that the chances of an unchurched person being invited to attend a church by someone who frequents one are diminishing.

The general awareness of religious institutions among Americans is deteriorating. We asked a national sample of

98

unchurched people to identify the names of religious institutions and denominations with which they were familiar. The results were amazing. The most frequently named denomination was the Catholic church, mentioned by slightly more than half of the unchurched adults (56%). Next on the list were Baptist churches (34%), Jewish synagogues (22%), the "Christian church" (18%), the equally generic "Protestant church" (18%), Methodist (16%), Mormon (13%), and Lutheran (11%). No other denominations were named by at least 10%.

Look at that list. One denomination was recalled by at least half of the unchurched, only one more was remembered by at least one-quarter of the group, and only two other Protestant denominations were identified by at least one out of ten people. The Jewish synagogues of America, though serving just 2% of the population, were more likely to be recalled than were Methodist and Lutheran churches. Presbyterian churches were outpaced by the Mormon church. Jehovah's Witnesses and Muslim mosques had greater recall levels than did Episcopal churches. The Church of Christ, Assembly of God, Nazarene, and Church of God denominations did not make the radar screen.

The point of this recitation is not to applaud some churches and denigrate others. Frankly, these top-of-mind recall levels are appallingly small for organizations that have been around for decades and decades, have hundreds and hundreds of "franchises" around the nation, represent churches that spend billions of dollars each year, and have a mission that includes penetrating the community with their presence. The point is that Christian churches, of every shape and form, are losing their place in people's consciousness. There may have been a time in America's history when targeting a community and "hanging a shingle" would have been enough to attract a core group upon which the church could be founded and expanded. Today, denominational names and distinctions are meaningless to most people— unchurched or churched. Even knowing that there are a plethora of churches operating within the community is lost knowledge.

So what will it take to restore people's awareness of the church choices and distinctives that reside right under their noses? Let's consider the information about a church that matters the most to them, the communications that influence their thinking and choices, and the role of personal relationships in reaching the unchurched.

KEY FACTORS IN THEIR CHOICE

When unchurched people are seeking information about a church, or which churches to visit, they pay attention to certain bits of insight and ignore other facts. Often, the information that people in the church think would be important turns out to be irrelevant in the reflections of the unchurched. You can see this in the responses shown in Table 8.1.

The unchurched are looking for evidence of real Christianity. To them, that is manifested in people within a church who truly love each other. Two-thirds said that is either extremely or very important to them when they evaluate whether or not they would like a church. Another indicator of value to them is the quality of the sermons. Importantly, they are not seeking moral truth as much as they are seeking personal relevance and a loving tone. (Keep in mind that they are not likely to think of biblical truth as the core of relevance; the real issue is how that truth is conveyed. We dare not compromise God's truth and principles, but we are likely to gain an audience with the unchurched only if the manner in which we convey those insights seems reasonable, compassionate, contemporary and personally applicable.)

Six out of ten unchurched people are also anxious to find a church that has theological beliefs and doctrinal stands that they deem palatable. Of course, when the unchurched talk about theology and doctrine, they are not talking about the fine points of soteriology, eschatology, or ecclesiology. Their scrutiny focuses on fundamental questions, such as: Do you believe in a literal interpretation of the Bible? Do you believe that Jesus is

God? What do you teach about forgiveness and eternity? Do you push tithing? What behaviors constitute sin in your system? In essence, they are seeking to figure out what part of the spiritual world you occupy: Protestantism, Catholicism, eastern mysticism, metaphysical groups, etc. The fine points of theology are not at stake here; they want to understand your overall leanings.

Six out of ten are also very interested in being associated with a church that helps the poor and disadvantaged people of their community. Our work has shown that unchurched adults are striving to identify the heart of the people in the congregation more than they are seeking out opportunities to personally get involved. Again, their objective is to discover evidence of the authenticity of the people's faith commitment.

About half of the unchurched said that the quality of the programs and classes for children was of great importance to them. Among the unchurched who actually have children under 18, this was the single, most important item of all: seven out of ten rated it as either "extremely" or "very" important. Among unchurched adults who do not have children, this was one of the lowest-rated factors tested.

Let's stop here for a moment. Realize that of the dozen factors we tested, these were the only ones that at least half of the unchurched said were important to them. Keep in mind, of course, that there was no "cost" associated with saying that any of these factors was critically important. Consequently, the fact that the other items on the list were not listed as highly significant is, in itself, highly significant.

The items that were comparatively less important included being personally impressed with someone they know who attends the church; the quality of the church's worship music; a personal invitation or recommendation from someone they know; the denominational affiliation of the church; the distance of the church from their home; the evangelistic fervor of the congregation; and the church's level of social and political action.

Upon comparing the current findings with those from past years, we find a few patterns that can be explained by related insights into current cultural change. For instance, although the church's theology and doctrine remain quite important to people, the relative importance of that content has declined substantially in the past decade. This fits with the trend of homogenized theology and substantive tolerance: it doesn't matter what you believe as long as you believe something, and it is more important for you to be accepting of others' views than for you to be right. In an environment in which there is no absolute moral truth, the existence of belief transcends the importance of the substance of those beliefs.

Denominational affiliation is also less important to people than it was in 1990–and, even then, it was less significant to people than it had been two decades earlier. This, too, fits the trend in our culture: people matter, institutions don't. As Americans assess who they are, who they want to be, and how they wish to be perceived by others, the chances of them shaping their character and image to integrate the values and nature of a macro-level institution, such as a denomination, are declining. We have noticed during the Nineties that fewer and fewer people describe themselves as "Presbyterian" or "Lutheran" or "Methodist," for instance, but instead simply say they are "Christian," "Protestant" or "spiritual."

TABLE 8.1
THE IMPORTANCE OF DIFFERENT FACTORS TO THE UNCHURCHED WHEN THEY SELECT A CHURCH TO VISIT

HOW IMPORTANT IS THIS FACTOR?	extremely	very	only somewhat	not too	not at all
how much the people in the church seem to care about each other	46%	20%	22%	4%	9%
the quality of the sermons	42	23	17	5	12
their theological beliefs and doctrine	41	20	19	6	11
how much the church is involved in helping the poor and disadvantaged	38	22	25	5	9
the quality of programs and classes for children	36	18	18	9	18
your impressions of the people you know who attend the church	19	20	30	12	17
the quality of the music in the services	19	18	28	12	23
denominational affiliation of the church	18	17	29	12	20
how committed the people in the church are to sharing their faith	15	10	29	15	29
a personal invitation or recommendation from someone you know and trust	14	22	31	14	17
how far the church is from your home	14	18	31	10	25
how much the church is involved in political and social issues	14	10	21	13	38

103

The mobility and adventuresome spirit of Americans has led to factors such as the distance of a church from their home becoming less important. These days people will drive as far as they have to drive in order to have a good experience. It may be a relational experience, a spiritual experience, an entertainment experience or an intellectual experience, but experience rules in our culture. If it takes an extra few minutes or dollars to gain access to a superior experience, we deem it to be worthwhile.

GRABBING THEIR ATTENTION

Communications analysts estimate that the typical American is exposed to an average of 1500 to 2000 commercial and promotional messages every day. You are bombarded with commercials everywhere you turn: on license plate holders, coffee mugs, pens, the sides of trucks, the first few minutes of movie rentals, even in church bulletins – anything that has public visibility is a potential ad space. The profusion of ads has made the ability to slice through the clutter one of the daunting challenges to modern communicators and marketers.

The typical church has a minimal budget for advertising and limited expertise in such forms of communication. How can churches hope to cut through the clutter to reach their desired audience and to hit home with a precise and compelling message? The answer lies partially in knowing how to target those communication efforts.

If you look at Table 8.2 you will find that only three out of the nine methods tested seem to have much pull with the unchurched–and all three of those methods depend on personal relationships. The greatest influence would be for a friend to invite the unchurched person to accompany them to church: two-thirds of the unchurched said that would have a positive effect. Just as importantly, notice that only one out of every twenty-five unchurched adults said that if they were invited to attend a church it would make them less likely to do so. We know from the earlier discussion in this book that unchurched people are less likely than churched people to be highly relational in nature. Even so, they are affected by the personal touch, especially when it comes from a friend whose judgment and sensitivity they trust.

Almost as impactful is when a pastor personally invites someone to attend the church. Even though that may be an expected, "professional" act coming from a pastor, people are likely to react positively to such an expression of personal interest. This approach is especially significant to Busters, who generally feel snubbed or undervalued by people in positions of authority or by older people, and to blacks, who still tend to regard pastors as the leaders of the black community and as individuals worthy of respect.

Believers ought to be careful regarding the things they say about their church when they are in public. The surveys we conducted show that one of the most powerful influences on an unchurched person's behavior is what they hear from their friends about the life of a church. (We also discovered that when churched people talk about significant changes made at a church to make its ministry more relevant, almost half of the unchurched people exposed to such conversation are more likely to consider attending that church.)

Two things must be said about the use of traditional marketing media, such as print advertising, broadcasting, telemarketing and direct mail. First, none of those approaches has enough impact, in most cases, to justify the costs involved in the efforts. The people most likely to be attentive to the communications are already churched, which means that if the message is successful in bringing people to the church being promoted, all it has done is steal people from other churches. Meanwhile, the unchurched – the real target audience – pay little attention.

Second, in comparing the ability of these media to reach the unchurched to their ability to do so ten years ago, a huge change has taken place. In 1990, the unchurched were active consumers of such contacts, although not always for the better (i.e. some church media efforts actually made them less likely to attend the church). The big issue today is widespread indifference to communications. As you can see in Table 8.2, the dominant reaction to most church-based communication efforts is indifference. Ten years ago, people were likely to be incensed by a telephone call from a telemarketer on behalf of a church. Times have changed. Today, they're more likely to immediately hang up (if the call penetrates their call screening or answering machine) without giving it a second thought. Ten years ago, consumers scrutinized every piece of mail that came their way, even overt junk mail. Today, a growing number of pieces of mail never get to the "opened" stage, much less to the "read before discarded" stage. Making an impression on consumers is several-fold more difficult than it was just ten years ago. The methods that work best are those that are most personal.

TABLE 8.2
PRIME MEDIA FOR
MARKETING YOUR CHURCH
(impact of communication methods on
the likelihood of attending a church)

	impact upon likelihood of attending a church:			
	a lot more	little more	makes no difference	less
invited by a friend or neighbor	27%	36%	32%	4%
invited by the pastor	22	28	40	6
heard good things about the church from a friend	21	27	47	4
received a telephone call inviting you to attend	8	19	49	21
saw or heard a broadcast of the church's worship services	7	14	60	16
received a mailed flyer/brochure	6	14	61	18
saw a television ad for the church	5	11	63	20
church name sounds appealing	4	7	77	10
saw an ad for the church in the newspaper or Yellow Pages	3	6	74	16

Some churches have tried to expand and exploit the name recognition of their senior pastor as a means of building the church's constituency. The assumption is that because he/she has prayed at local events, has sent mailers to households throughout the community and has served on community task forces, people will know and respect the pastor. Involvement in those types of activities may have built a high profile for a pastor in the 1950s, but times have changed. No matter how well-known and highly respected you think the pastor of your church is, chances are good that most of the people in your area are not aware of him/her. Here are several illustrations of that concept.

You are probably aware of Charles Swindoll, Gary Smalley, Beverly LaHaye, and Josh McDowell. They each have had extensive media ministries and best-selling books. They have been newsmakers for years and have spoken to thousands upon thousands of people. Born again Christians all over America are familiar with their names, their faces and their ministry efforts. But not one of them is known to even one out of every twenty unchurched adults.

The pastor of one of the largest and best-known churches in America is Bill Hybels, of Willow Creek Community Church outside of Chicago. Hybels has authored books that have topped the charts of the Christian bestsellers. Audio tapes of his sermons sell by the thousands. The conferences held at Willow Creek each year, featuring Hybels and other speakers, sell out within weeks of being announced. He has been a counselor to the President and has started an international association of "seeker" churches. He has been called the most influential pastor in America. Hybels is known by fewer than one out of four churched people, and by less than 3% of the unchurched.

James Dobson has been hosting the *Focus on the Family* program for more than a quarter century. His show is heard on more than 1500 radio stations every day. His books and videos have sold millions of copies. He has faithfully served presidents, congressional committees and national family-policy study groups for years. His organization is visited by tens of thousands of people every year, and contacted by hundreds of thousands. The variety of magazines they produce for targeted audiences – including adolescents, teenagers, parents, pastors, doctors, teachers and grandparents – are read by millions of families and individuals. When Christian marketers want to get the endorsement of a highly respected, well-known Christian figure, Dr. Dobson is one of the names high on the list. And yet, fewer than one out of every five unchurched adults have ever heard of James Dobson.

Using individuals from your church, such as a pastor or other "celebrities" from your community to raise peoples awareness of, and interest in, your church is a difficult strategy to employ successfully. Think twice before you embark on this path. Few churches have used it to their advantage.

POSITIONING THE CHURCH

The choice of messages that the church delivers to its target audience also makes a difference in the ability to affect people's attitudes and behavior. The choices are seemingly endless, but our limited evaluation of even a few, simple positioning points shows the importance of knowing how you want to be thought of, and then effectively conveying information that fosters that image.

Consistent with other findings from our research we discovered that of the seven descriptions tested, the approach that was most appealing to the unchurched was indicating that the church is actively involved in helping poor and disadvantaged people. Half of the unchurched said that positioning made a church "very appealing" and another one-third said it made a church "somewhat appealing." This image was especially appealing to women, downscale individuals and black adults.

The next most attractive positioning was to communicate that the church is meeting the needs of the entire family unit. About two out of five adults said this made a church very appealing, and one-third said it made the church somewhat appealing. Nearly identical results were derived when we asked about positioning a church as concerned about the declining morals of American society.

Being known as a place that was helping people to apply Christianity in their daily lives was slightly less appealing to people, but still drew positive reaction from a majority. Lesser appeal was associated with being positioned as a church that is "relevant for your life today" or being "biblically based." By far the least appealing image was being a church that is politically active. Only one out of ten adults said that such an image made the church very appealing, and two out of ten stated that such a church would be somewhat appealing to them. Most significantly, half of the unchurched said that a church that prides itself on being politically active would be "not at all appealing" to them.

Various niches within the unchurched population expressed atypical preferences. For instance, Builders (people in their mid-fifties to early seventies) were more likely to be drawn to a church that is said to be biblically based, concerned about moral decline, and focused on applicable Christianity. The skepticism of the upscale constituency (i.e. people with college degrees and above-average incomes) was evident: across-the-board, they were less likely than were other adults to find any of these positioning statements to make a church more appealing. Blacks adults were especially influenced by hearing that a church is helping the needy and that it seeks to facilitate faith applications.

ARE WE EXPLOITING THE OPPORTUNITIES?

Without a doubt, one of the most important strategies to employ in influencing the unchurched is for their trusted friends to invite them to attend church. This is not a new idea. For at least half a century, proponents of church growth have described the significance of "friendship evangelism," personal relationships, and marketing through word-of-mouth.

How are we doing at following through on this known principle? According to the unchurched, one out of four of them have been asked to attend a church service or church event with a friend in the past 12 months. Of those, one out of every seven attended. In other words, if we look at the aggregate body of unchurched adults, 4% were invited to attend church with a friend and did so; 23% were invited to attend, but declined; and 73% were never invited. What does this tell us?

Perhaps the most obvious observation is that most unchurched people are not being pursued by anyone. We outnumber them two to one. We are called by God to pursue them. We spend more than $3 billion every year in America constructing or renovating church facilities in which to host them. But the single most effective strategy of all – following Jesus, lead of asking them to "come and see" – is generally neglected.

FEW ARE ASKED TO ATTEND, EVEN FEWER COME

How Many Unchurched Were Personally Invited to a Church – and Attended – in the Past 12 Months?

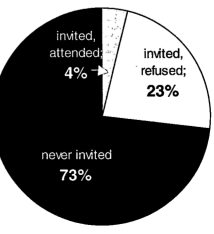

invited, attended; 4%

invited, refused; 23%

never invited 73%

A second observation is that we have to be prepared for rejection. Almost nine out of ten of the unchurched people who were invited refused to go. But things may not be quite this bleak. Realize that we were interviewing the unchurched. What about the formerly unchurched who were invited, attended and have since remained connected to the life of a church? We do not have figures on the size of that group, but it would reduce the rejection statistics by some margin. Even so, rejection is a very real possibility when we attempt to lead a friend back to the church. That is simply one of the breaks of the game; we cannot let it deter us from engaging them and seeking to help them enjoy church life.

So What?

Some things never change. One of those things seems to be the ways by which unchurched people make their way back to the church. As much as at any time in the last 15 years, the key to drawing them back remains relationships and invitations. They do not come if we do not ask.

The unchurched have been there, done that, heard it all. They are not going to be drawn to a church because of the size of the congregation, its history, the genius of the pastor, the talent of the musicians, or the convenience of freeway access. Those things don't hurt, necessarily, but they are not what ring the bells of the unchurched. They need to see a group of people who cares about each other and about those who are in need. They need to sense the relevance of the church – but it must be conveyed by example, not by proclamation of being relevant. And there must be something different about the church. The message and the experience, then, must be compelling, convincing, and consistent; anything less gets lost in the cacophony of self-promotional noise that we endure day in and day out.

How ironic it is that in this age of complexity, it is the simplest of strategies – asking someone to attend – that has the greatest power. However, our research highlights a harsh reality about the process of inviting the unchurched to accompany us to church: they will usually reject our offer. Perhaps the most intriguing reality is that they are rarely offended by a reasonable, well-intentioned request. Therefore, it may take us several attempts at bringing them to a church before they are ready to do so. We can neither be shy nor lack perseverance. While those offers must be made sensibly and sensitively, as people see things in us and hear things about our churches that are attractive, the odds of them accompanying us become better. (Remember, too, that in their eyes, attending a worship service is rarely the ideal initial introduction to a church.)

As we discuss our church history and relationship with unchurched friends, bear in mind that they are more interested in having a positive experience than in learning accurate Bible content. The latter may be a highly defensible reason for pursuing them; the former may be the most plausible means of reaching them. Striking a viable balance is part of the art of influencing the unchurched to give organized religion another try.

Although the research clearly shows that most unchurched people do not go to church because of a radio commercial, mailed brochure or newspaper ad – and there are ample numbers of churches across America whose experience verifies that – the mass media may still be a useful weapon in your marketing arsenal. If the media can be used to support other outreach efforts – that is, as a secondary rather than primary thrust – then it may justify its cost. The most recent craze in advertising circles has been to achieve "message integration," meaning that the product or service advertised is supported by a multi-faceted campaign in which all of the communications vehicles utilized are integrated in message, tone, offer and measurement. The notion of weaving together all of your church's efforts to penetrate the unchurched bears further consideration.

Nine

TWELVE
MISCONCEPTIONS
ABOUT MINISTRY TO
THE UNCHURCHED

One of the most interesting facets of the research we conduct is the ability to distinguish fact from fiction in regard to the aspect of ministry we are studying. Often, as we research a ministry topic, we discover that there are myths believed by substantial numbers of people. Not surprisingly, as we evaluated the philosophy, process and ministry outcomes of the churches that are doing some of the most effective ministry to the unchurched throughout the U.S., we found a number of inconsistencies between what many believe about reaching the unchurched and how it really works. Because the acceptance of such myths can undermine our ability to have a positive impact in people's lives, let's spend this chapter identifying twelve common misconceptions regarding ministering to the unchurched. Hopefully, awareness of these misconceptions will lead to the elimination of incorrect thinking and ineffective practices, thereby improving the quality of future outreach efforts.

MISCONCEPTION #1
SUCCESSFUL MINISTRY TO THE UNCHURCHED DEPENDS ON FOLLOWING THE RIGHT MODEL.

Our national surveys among pastors indicate that most of them have a program or formulaic mentality about reaching unchurched people. Their notion is that reaching the unchurched and affecting their lives is no different than any other program: identify the niche, develop a needs-solving activity, systematize it, and then move the participants to the next level of spiritual maturity.

Our study of the churches that are doing stellar work among the unchurched revealed a completely different mindset. Ministry to unchurched people is about developing a culture within the church, not a program. Evangelism is not an activity but a lifestyle in these churches. For that lifestyle to be embraced by the congregation it must be modeled by the pastoral staff and lay leaders for everyone to see and appreciate. We saw that if a church wants to be truly evangelistic and attract unchurched people, it must do more than have a contemporary worship service or change the language it uses to exorcise the Elizabethan terms and insider lingo that baffle the unchurched. It must change the hearts of its own people so that they become passionate about reaching folks who have no connection with Christ. That has little to do with the "Willow Creek model" or the "Saddleback model."

MISCONCEPTION #2
THE BIGGEST PROBLEM IN SUCH A MINISTRY WILL BE DEALING WITH THE ATTITUDES OF THE UNCHURCHED TOWARD CHRISTIANITY AND CHURCHES.

Many pastors and believers assume that the toughest element in reaching the unchurched is changing their perceptions and attitudes about the Christian faith or about the value of church. Often, we assume that they possess contempt for the church and are stubborn in their refusal to see anything good about the Church.

The pastors of the model churches we studied have arrived at a different conclusion. The people with the attitude problem are more likely to be the churched Christians. Granted, there is a contingent of unchurched people who cannot even force themselves to think a civil thought about Christianity or churches. But they are not going to set foot in a church, anyway. The millions of unchurched individuals who do return to churches to check them out are more open-minded and malleable than we sometimes give them credit for. The more audacious task is getting churched people to genuinely care about the souls and the lives of those visitors. Getting them to give up their close-to-the-door parking spaces, to take time to get to know the newcomers, to ante up the money it takes to carry the costs of reaching out to those folks, or to get excited about a church that is not necessarily designed exclusively to meet their personal needs is often a major challenge. It's one thing to talk about the importance of capturing the hearts of wayward sinners for Christ, but it's another thing altogether to make the sacrifices necessary to accomplish that end.

MISCONCEPTION #3:
YOU MUST HAVE A SEEKER SERVICE.

Willow Creek Community Church popularized the notion of having a weekend service that is not a worship service, per se, but is specifically designed to attract and help unchurched people. It contains some of the elements of a typical worship service – most notably, music and a teaching time – but those elements have been refined to eliminate the expectation that an unchurched person would worship a God that he/she does not know. Instead, the service is developed to expose them to the relevance of the Bible, to positive thoughts about Christianity, to the friendliness of church people, and to an environment in which they feel welcome, comfortable and helped.

In our sample of the congregations most effective at reaching the unchurched, few offer a seeker service. Most of them provide full-on worship services that have been cleansed of "churchy" language, pipe organs, formal dress and traditional symbols (although those seem to be making a comeback, given the predispositions of Busters and Mosaics). These are churches that want unchurched people to be in a place of worship, while worship is happening. "There has to be a place for someone who is skeptical or unconvinced to see and experience Jesus for who He is. And the best place for that is in the context of corporate worship," was how one young pastor described it. His church has grown from zero to 2000 adults in seven years; almost two-thirds of them were unchurched at the time they first visited that church. "To us, there's something about not only God's presence being there, but also the community functioning in love and faith, that allows Jesus to encounter someone in a way that they're probably not going to encounter elsewhere."

A number of the pastors indicated that their services are seeker-sensitive, not seeker-driven. "What we do may seem like it was designed for seekers, but it wasn't. Believers live in the same world as the unchurched, so the style of music and communication that connects well with the followers of Christ is likely to connect with those who are not yet following him, too. The sensitivity to unchurched people is more likely to emerge in other ways." This Midwestern pastor of a mid-sized church described ways such as how the welcoming, follow-up, child care, parking, and post-service interaction are handled as examples of how they fine-tune the process to incorporate the unchurched.

MISCONCEPTION #4
THE BEST WAY TO ATTRACT THE UNCHURCHED IS THROUGH LARGE-SCALE EVENTS.

About half of the model churches use large-scale events to attract unchurched people. However, about half of those churches use them to build name awareness, develop relational bridges and create an image for their church. Only a couple of the effective churches we studied rely upon events to bring about change in the lives of the unchurched. Relatively few expect most of the individuals who attend the event to show up in church next Sunday. "We're establishing our presence, that's all," was how a pastor from a growing Baptist church in the South put it. "I can't reach them with radio or TV, but if I can give them a good time at a pleasant event, they'll remember us next time a friend mentions our church, or next time they pass our building. If they meet some good people and sense that we're really part of the community, not just a bunch of religious fanatics out to take away their fun and impose a bunch of rules, then we might have a shot at seeing them visit our church sometime. When they're ready."

Surprisingly, a number of the effective churches do not use events at all. One of the largest churches in Ohio, built primarily on reaching the unchurched, indicated that events are counter-productive to what they hope to achieve. "We're trying to create an approach of evangelism as a lifestyle. If we suddenly start relying on events, I send the wrong message to our people. We encourage people-building relationships, not handing out tickets to events, no matter how good they may be." Another pastor admitted that he sends people to the events put on by other churches. "It's not what we do. We're into building God's kingdom, so I don't need to have my own Easter show and Christmas special; if the church down the street does a great job at it, let's encourage people to take advantage of what they're doing. We have to focus on what makes us tick, and that's getting to know people and ministering on a one-to-one level."

MISCONCEPTION #5
THE ROUTE TO SUCCESS IS TO COPY WILLOW CREEK OR SADDLEBACK.

Most of the churches that are doing great work among the unchurched are very familiar with the work of these two groundbreaking churches. But not one church said that it uses either place as a model. "We're pretty eclectic," laughed a pastor from California. "We steal from everybody. Willow has some great stuff and we've adapted a few things from them. Saddleback has some wonderful ideas, too, and we've ripped off a few things from them. But we read a lot, we talk to our visitors, we're out in the community, we go to conferences – I mean, there's no single source of insight on this stuff for us."

While the leaders of the most effective churches for the unchurched revere pioneers like Bill Hybels and Rick Warren, they also recognize the limitations of blindly copying what has worked in other places, in different contexts. The principles and materials developed by the two giant churches are studied and adapted. The flattery by imitation stops at that point.

MISCONCEPTION #6
IF YOU DO IT RIGHT, MOST OF THE PEOPLE IN YOUR CHURCH WILL HAVE BEEN UNCHURCHED BEFORE THEY CHOSE YOURS AS THEIR HOME CHURCH.

Nationwide, less than 20% of all church growth is conversion growth. Transfer and biological means are responsible for the bulk of the growth counted by churches. Although the proportion of growth attributable to reaching the unchurched is much higher at churches that best reach and keep the unchurched, even in most of those places a majority of the growth is not attributable to reaching outsiders. Among the great churches we identified and studied vis-à-vis their ministry to the unchurched, the average number of current attenders who were previously unchurched was in the 40% to 50% range.

My intent is not to criticize or make light of that statistic. When you study this process and the people we hope to reach, and think about getting almost half of your people from the pool of Americans who are living apart from the organized faith world, you stand in awe of churches that can pull that off. But it's also important to see that even under the best of circumstances – leaders that are passionate about reaching the unchurched, a church culture that facilitates reaching them, a ministry that is focused on attracting and retaining them – a majority of the people that adopt a church as their own are coming from other churches.

For what it's worth, this is not all bad, either. As our interviews with the pastors and leaders of the effective churches highlighted, you need an army of believers who grasp the vision of penetrating the unchurched population and make it their life's mission. Some of the churches we spoke to that want to do this ministry have been thwarted in their efforts not by the lack of pastoral leadership, vision, or a big enough pool of unchurched people to draw from, but by the absence of enough believers who are excited about such a ministry. If the numerical growth occurring at your church is comprised of people who understand the vision for reaching the unchurched, and those newcomers want to sign on for that purpose, then you have a key part of the infrastructure necessary – i.e., human capital – to get the job done.

MISCONCEPTION #7
IF YOU DO A GOOD JOB, MOST OF YOUR UNCHURCHED VISITORS WILL RETURN.

We all hate rejection. Our natural reaction is to take it personally and to wonder what is wrong with us that caused other people to choose behaviors or lifestyles other than those that we have adopted and have made accessible to them. When it comes to reaching the unchurched, when a person visits our church but does not return, we interpret that as failure: their refusal to come back is viewed as a sign that we are doing something wrong.

Our evaluation of the ministries that are most effective at reaching the unchurched showed that they are also pretty effective at retaining them, but that even in these churches a majority of the unchurched that visit will not ultimately stay at the church. The range of unchurched visitors who did *not* return was from 30% to 70%; on average, about half came only once or a few times, then vanished. For many of the "best practices" churches, we found that a majority of the unchurched don't adopt the church as part of their life.

Given that we are talking about the most effective churches, that feels like a pretty high "rejection rate." The lesson in those numbers, though, is that not everyone who tries your church is going to feel comfortable there and choose it as their spiritual touchstone. Their decision to not embrace your church does not necessarily mean you are failing in your mission. We are striving to get the unchurched to make a major transition in their thinking and behavior; change may be the defining characteristic of our culture, but it still comes with great struggle to the individuals within that culture. If you want to succeed in reaching the unchurched, the sad fact is that growth is, in crass terms, a numbers game: even in response to your best efforts, some will walk away unconvinced. Having a tender heart and a tough skin are two necessary tools to begin and sustain this type of outreach.

MISCONCEPTION #8
MINISTRY TO THE UNCHURCHED TAKES A LARGE STAFF.

Several of the most effective churches started out trying to staff up in order to handle the needs of large numbers of unchurched people. Most of them gave up and realized the only way to be successful in ministering to significant numbers of unchurched people is when the laity of the congregation assume the role of minister. Said one pastor: "We found out that we just could not raise enough money to pull it off because when this is working, a large percentage of your congregation is unchurched and they do not give much money and they consume a huge amount of resources. Our only hope was to improve the servant attitude and activity of the members." This pastor described the struggle of finding the proper balance between hiring paid professionals to do ministry and equipping the laity to be effective avocational ministers.

Ultimately, a church that is serious about reaching unchurched people may wish to have an individual on staff whose primary function is strategizing, organizing and supervising the efforts to reach that target group. However, most of the churches we studied did not stress out over having unique staff positions dedicated to unchurched ministry. "Our culture focuses on bringing unchurched people into our family. That's everyone's responsibility, within the context of every ministry function that takes place here," an associate pastor at one of the leading churches told us. "Everyone on staff is always conscious of the needs of the unchurched when they conceive and carry out their ministry. We don't have a 'pastor to the unchurched' because we all carry that as a sub-function or subconscious emphasis within our dominant frame of ministry–you know, discipleship, worship, or whatever."

MISCONCEPTION #9
THE UNCHURCHED REQUIRE ANONYMITY. WHEN THEY ARE READY TO GET INVOLVED, THEY'LL TELL YOU.

My reason for including this notion in the "misconceptions" category is not because it is wrong. The unchurched usually do require anonymity. When they are ready to make a deeper commitment, they will let you know. They don't want to feel coerced into anything. However, I was surprised at how aggressive the effective churches are at facilitating a commitment among the unchurched.

Frankly, everything hinges on the unchurched individual somehow identifying herself, usually by filling out a visitor's communication card during a service. Once that contact information is provided, the church springs into action, employing an intentional and strategic process designed to inform, encourage and motivate the visitor to move forward in the spiritual quest. This process usually includes a series of letters and postcards, one or two telephone calls, and an invitation to attend a one or two session class for newcomers. The key to success is not the actual steps but the tone of the process. This is not an insensitive play for warm bodies, but an energetic effort to let unchurched individuals know what is available to them and the process and implications of making a deeper commitment. These churches do not push the person into a commitment; some tried that, and realized that it quickly raised the defenses or fears of the unchurched. Control must remain in the hands of the unchurched individual. The church simply lets the person know that the church cares, the church has ministries of value, and that there is an easy and minimally threatening process by which they can get into the mainstream of the church.

MISCONCEPTION #10
IF AN UNCHURCHED PERSON COMES FIVE OR SIX TIMES, THEY'LL STAY FOR GOOD.

This makes sense: coming a half dozen times to a church demonstrates continued interest and the willingness to change existing behavioral patterns. Unfortunately, even if they come five or six times, they are not necessarily sold on what the church is all about.

The key is to go beyond having people attend and observe to having them attend and get involved. Once a person finds some type of connection point – a class or program to attend, a means of serving – then they are likely to feel they are part of the church. The bottom line is being relationally connected.

Unless they are woven into a tapestry of meaningful or satisfying relationships, it is not unusual for a person to come to worship services six, seven or even eight times, then disappear. Typically, an unchurched person who identifies a fulfilling niche in their first or second visit is more likely to remain in the church than a person who attends seven or eight times but is not interpersonally connected.

MISCONCEPTION #11
SUCCESS IN REACHING THE UNCHURCHED DEPENDS ON THE PASTOR'S PERSONALITY AND PREACHING.

If you want to attract unchurched people to your church, it helps if the pastor has a charismatic personality and delivers clear and stirring sermons on topics of interest, with practical applications. But that would not be enough to attract and retain the unchurched.

According to the leaders of the churches that are doing effective ministry among the unchurched, the environment of the church and the attitude and spiritual commitment of the congregants are more important than the pastor and the preaching. "You can't really fool people into thinking you care if you don't," one pastor told us. "They've seen that a hundred times before. They're really sensitive to it." Becoming part of a church is about developing an entirely new network of relationships and emotional connections. That's a big step for people; they move into it cautiously, especially those who have been disappointed by churches in the past.

"It took me a while, but I realized that I could stand up there and preach heresy for weeks on end and they either wouldn't care or didn't know the difference." This was a pastor of a growing church in the Midwest, speaking from his experience. "What they *did* notice was how the people treated each other, how comfortable they felt in our place, and what their kids said about their experience. They didn't want a lot of generic religious platitudes. Really, they weren't sure what they were looking for, but they'd experienced what they knew they *weren't* looking for. I'm not saying preaching doesn't matter, only that to the unchurched, it doesn't matter as much as some of the other things they experience."

As several pastors took great pains to point out – and rightly so – any success we experience in reaching the unchurched has more to do with allowing the Holy Spirit to work than it relies upon our own skills and cleverness. One pastor stated it this way: "Once I've done what I can to set the stage, I just have to get out of the way and let the Holy Spirit do His thing. That's what keeps people – when they experience the touch of God."

MISCONCEPTION #12
ONCE YOU START ATTRACTING THEM, THE CHALLENGE IS SIMPLY MANAGING THE FLOW OF INCOMING UNCHURCHED.

Many pastors seem to believe that once you tap into the unchurched population, the word gets out and there is no stopping them from coming. Then, the challenge becomes management rather than marketing.

As our sample of pastors leading the most effective churches explained it, there is definitely some momentum that is generated once you begin to attract unchurched people, but there is no guarantee that such people will continue to stream into the church. "It's not like the unchurched are a community, or anything," laughed one pastor serving an evangelical church in the southwest. "You have to stick to the fundamentals that got some of them coming in the first place."

The bigger issue, according to most of these church leaders, is not managing the newcomers, but raising the resources to keep the ministry going. "I have an awfully tough time trying to find enough mature believers to mentor or teach or serve newcomers. Coming into this I knew that it would be tough to balance the resource mix–and even then, I really underestimated what it takes." This pastor's church grew by 1000 people in less than three years, placing an incredible strain on the ministry. "But that's why we started this thing – we wanted to reach those people. Our problem is how to take proper care of them when they get here. And that's an issue with the churched people, not the unchurched. What happens when God answers our prayers and the unchurched come – and come, and come, and come? That's when it's time for believers to really step up to the plate and get the job done. That's what puts your heart to the test: are you really willing to do what it takes to guide these people to the next step?"

Obviously, ministry to the unchurched is a bit different than you might have assumed. Are any of these misconceptions at work in your ministry?

Ten

HOW CHURCHES MINISTER EFFECTIVELY TO THE UNCHURCHED

O̲ur research among churches that are doing a superb job at reaching and retaining the unchurched was quite revealing. Let me share some of the key insights with you. But let me make a few introductory comments that set the stage for understanding how and why these churches are so effective in their ministry to the unreached.

First, all of these churches have a senior pastor who is driven to embrace people who are not in love with God. Whether you call it a gift, a passion or a calling, each pastor was unquestionably and unshakably committed to helping grow the kingdom by attracting outsiders. Some of them were obviously brilliant; some were not. Some of them were charismatic; some were not. Some of them were experienced pastors; some were novices serving in their first church. But God's love and His vision, instilled within the hearts of these men (I'm not being sexist - all of the pastors of these churches happened to be male, as is true of 96% of Protestant churches) was clear.

Second, a firm understanding of the scriptural imperative to reach the unreached supported each church's efforts. The pastors and staff we interviewed cited different passages of the Bible that moved them, but all of them referred to God's Word as the fundamental motivation for pursuing the hard-to-reach.

Third, in every church, this ministry was a church-wide crusade, not the pastor's pet project. The goal was to have everyone in the congregation intentionally building bridges to unchurched people, and eventually inviting those individuals to the church. Even the new churches we studied were characterized by the founding pastor enlisting the participation of a few core individuals who shared a passion for reaching unreached individuals. The philosophy was that this effort must be the driving purpose of the church, and not just an ancillary ministry.

With that in mind, let's identify some of the keys to effective church-based ministry to the unchurched. Note that every one of the two-dozen churches we studied in greater detail operates differently than every other one. What I will describe for you are the common philosophies and activities they share, the "best practices," if you will, of the churches that are leading the way in penetrating the one-third of America's population that is disconnected from the Church.

BEST PRACTICES: PHILOSOPHY OF MINISTRY

The underlying purpose of these churches is clear to all who participate in the church: to love people into the kingdom of God. While these churches are cognizant of numbers, they are more concerned about hearts and souls than attendance figures; reaching the unchurched is not just a numbers game. "I'd rather see ten people come to the Lord and really grow into maturity than have an auditorium filled with happy faces but empty souls," said the pastor of a church in Iowa. These are churches that focus on building God's kingdom, not the pastor's kingdom or the church's turf. The pastor of a Baptist church in Texas that regularly attracts 1500 adults described his view. "One of the things we've learned is God blesses your church with growth when you're not selfish about wanting to keep all of those people inside your building. It's amazing how God takes care of that!"

Using Scripture as the foundation, these churches also have a keen sense of the necessity of the Holy Spirit doing the brunt of the work. The church, through its efforts and attitudes, creates an environment in which God can impact the minds and hearts of unchurched people. "When they come here, our goal is for them to sense the presence of God. We want every single person that comes in to respond to and connect with God," said one pastor. "It goes back to an old philosophy: the Holy Spirit will work in every single person we touch. The Holy Spirit led that person to our church because God wants to get to know them. We really want people to connect with God."

The laser-like focus of these churches is impossible to miss. Have you ever heard the expression "to a hammer, everything looks like a nail?" That's what these churches are like: to them, every unchurched person looks like a human being just waiting to have a transforming experience with God. Even the language they use to describe the unchurched – pre-Christians, people who don't yet realize God loves them, soon-to-be-Christians – reflects that view. "Evangelism is really the only thing we can do better here on earth than we will in Heaven," opined one pastor. "Once we get saved, it becomes our primary purpose for existence." Another pastor echoed the same sentiment. "When you boil it all down, we do two things: evangelize and disciple people. So we create a place where God can work through us to do those things." It's not that these individuals ignore the significance of worship, stewardship or community service; they simply see evangelism and discipleship as the priorities, and everything else flows from those two foci.

Reaching the unchurched demands a persistent effort to remain culturally aware and relevant. "We continue to ask questions," a pastor explained about their ability to remain attractive to the unchurched. "This isn't a 'done' thing for us, and I don't think it ever will be. It's very dynamic. Society just keeps changing, so we have to stay in touch with the culture. We have to be willing to 'de-weird' the church."

That also means that a church's activities will be constantly changing and shifting to remain in-step with the culture. One of the refreshing attitudes of the pastors we interviewed was their determination to continually experiment and to refuse to lock into one set approach. "We do whatever it takes," was the philosophy of the pastor of a church in Texas that has grown large and is pioneering a variety of new approaches to reaching people, such as starting mini-churches in retirement villages and apartment complexes, as well as planting ethnic churches throughout the city. "We try all means to get someone in. We're willing to try anything."

Constant change also means challenging one's prevailing assumptions about almost everything. Conditions that used to be taken for granted are up for grabs these days, so leaders have to be wary of falling into routines and ruts – even if those routines were trailblazing ten years ago. Pastors have even questioned the viability of building on basic knowledge that was once a safe assumption. "We're finding more and more people who have no Christian background, where even five or ten years ago everybody had grown up going to Sunday school, or the church down the street, or a Vacation Bible School." This pastor leads a contemporary church in the middle of the South, and has had to identify and reassess even his most basic beliefs about what people know and how they think. "The thing that's been hard for me to adjust to is that there are people that, if I say 'When Adam and Eve did so and so,' then I've got to purposely stop and explain who Adam and Eve were. But that's just part of the art of reaching these people; you can't figure they're just like you are."

One of the approaches that all of these churches accept is the "steal and adapt" strategy. "Hey, if you look closely at what we're doing – well, you don't even have to look that closely – there's not a whole lot that we do that's original or stellar. I mean, we're not a pioneering church." This pastor leads an Evangelical Free church of 1300-plus adults in Michigan. He recognizes that a lifetime's worth of great ideas and ministry lessons are available to him from the other church leaders who share the same heartbeat to reach the unchurched. "We do some things well, we do some things poorly, and for some reason God has chosen to make this place explode, and so it does. We don't have secrets or hidden things that make us successful. We read constantly. We grab stuff from here and there. We tweak it a little here, twist it a little there, make it ours. But it's a collection of other people's stuff that we've just adapted, based on what they've learned and what we've experienced."

Sometimes that result is that the churched people lose their sense of comfort. One of the pastors, who heads a church in Alabama, responded, "The things we do put off some of my churched people, but we find that the unchurched say 'Hey, we really want to check out a place like that.' We built this place to reach the unchurched, so if anyone has to feel uncomfortable here, I'm okay with it being the churched folk. They'll find a place that will keep them happy."

The underlying assumption is that if people who attend a church are excited about it, then their conviction and enthusiasm – not marketing gimmicks, sermon series, free gifts or Broadway productions – will capture the attention of their unchurched friends. Said the Alabama pastor: "Bottom line? People like to go to church where somebody else likes to go to church. If people are going away from this place and gossiping that good things are happening here, that gets other folks interested. When church people get excited, other people want to know why."

The outreach director at a Lutheran church found the excitement principle to be key, too, but that it had to be authentic excitement, not manufactured, Sunday-only joy. "I was in a church where we had a 40-foot stretch between the door to the worship center and the doorway into the sanctuary. We established a rule that a visitor needed to be greeted at least four times before they got into that sanctuary. And it worked! They were greeted every ten feet. Except there was one little problem: that wasn't what the culture of the church was *really* like. Most of the people just stood along the outer walls of the church, they weren't enthusiastic about new people joining us. So, a visitor would enter, get a warm and friendly greeting several times, and think, 'This is a pretty good church, let's join.' For a few weeks, until they become known, they were treated nicely and greeted warmly, but then they became part of the familiar crowd. They sort of settled in and all of a sudden they're looking around wondering 'What happened? Now I'm not important anymore?' And it was because we created a false culture. The people who really were the heart of the church just weren't interested in them. We had created a false façade to the church and it was really harmful."

Most of the pastors we spoke to discussed the importance of the heart of the people. "It's all about people. Your people have to have a heart to see others come to know Jesus and to connect with those people. You can do without books and tapes and seminars, but you can't make this kind of ministry happen without people that have that heart."

Perhaps more than anything else, ministry to the unchurched hinges on one core factor: relationships. This point was driven home to one pastor through the comments of some people who recently visited his church. "Yeah, it's funny because for five or six years we did radio advertising. Some of those people who heard the ads are coming now. But they never came when all they heard were the radio spots. Now, because a friend asked them to come, they're here. I ask them 'When did you first hear about our church?' and they'll say 'Oh, I used to listen to your radio spots all the time.' But it wasn't the radio that brought them to church. It introduced them to the church, but they didn't come until years later when their friend invited them."

This insight was conveyed from a different angle by a Baptist pastor in northern California. "People don't want a friendly church. They want a friend. Systems don't work. You have to create ways to enable people to find a genuine friend." The underlying philosophy of these ministries is always that unless the people of the church truly care about the unchurched, and are willing to make the sacrifices for those relationships to occur, the ministry is headed for disaster.

BEST PRACTICES: PREPARATION

A great ministry to the unchurched doesn't just happen. Such a ministry is not only the result of a clear, thoughtful and well-articulated philosophy, but also a commitment to adequate preparation of the congregation to accomplish the daunting but rewarding task at hand. The pastors of these churches have worked long and hard to get people in the right frame of mind so that the ministry isn't a bunch of programs, but a group of loving people who really care about the spiritual health of others. They want their people to be always thinking about building relationships with unchurched people. "It takes a long time for that to become part of their mindset," cautioned one senior pastor. "Almost every week I weave the importance of sensitivity and reaching out and making friendships into the message and into our announcements. It's so easy for people to revert to their old ways. They need continual reminders that the old ways are not what we're about, not what God has called us to."

The goal is that when the churched invite the unchurched to accompany them to a service or other activity, that invitation is satisfying an expectation, not serving as an exception. The relationships remove one of the big hurdles for churches to overcome: isolation and the fear of remaining disconnected.

But the people have to be prepared to discuss their faith, too. "If my people encounter an individual who is not a believer, but really wants to know what this stuff is all about, I don't want them running to the church to drag the evangelism director out there to share the gospel. That's why we don't have an evangelism director; every person in this place is an evangelism director."

So apologetics is one focus within the church. "But that word is so ... sophisticated!," retorted one pastor. "It's not really high-level stuff we're dealing with here. My people need to be ready to address all kinds of theological garbage that the unchurched have unwittingly bought into over the years. My people have to be prepared to give a clear and articulate reason for the hope and faith that is within them. We're not talking the Mannheim Lectures here, we're talking about being able to communicate the basic stories of the Bible and relate them to everyday life."

Having a strong ministry to the unchurched also takes resources. We found that these places intentionally and strategically budget funds to do this work. On average, perhaps 20% of the annual church budget is geared to this specific process. (Several pastors demurred, stating that everything the church does is geared to the unchurched and therefore their entire budget fits this category.)

These churches have worked hard to provide many ways that an outsider can easily become an insider. While the worship service gets most of the attention, many of the pastors recognize that it all starts with relationships and perhaps other exposure to the faith world before the unchurched individual sets foot inside the worship center. "We joined the city sports leagues, we hold seminars, we do all kinds of bridging events. We know they're not going to be converted at those events – we don't even try, really. We just want them to know that we're nice, normal people, we struggle with the same issues, we have many of the same interests, but we have that little something extra – the Jesus factor –

that gives us the edge. I don't care how they catch that notion, as long as they want more and more of it to be revealed. So we try all kinds of avenues that allow them to enter into a relationship with us and with God."

Ultimately, the unchurched wind up attending a worship service, so these churches go to great lengths to ensure that the worship services are worshipful while also being accessible to people who have little or no church history. The choice of music – the lyrics, the instrumentation, the difficulty of the tunes – is important. The topics of the message and the language used are carefully examined. Integration of technology into the worship process – video clips, PowerPoint slides, excellent sound systems, good lighting – are part of the approach. The layout of the campus, signage, comfort of the seating, ease of parking – all of these elements and more are painstakingly examined and constantly refined since they are an integral part of the aggregate experience. It's all considered part of the preparation for guiding the unchurched to God while meeting the needs of the church family at the same time.

BEST PRACTICES: PROCESS

Successfully penetrating the ranks of the unchurched largely hinges on whether or not the congregants build credible relationships with people and then invite those friends to attend the church. This usually means visiting a worship service. In the effective churches, anywhere between 40% and 85% of the churched body actually invites non-believers to attend during a typical year.

Most of the effective churches strive to support their congregants in this effort by putting on anywhere between four and eight special events per year. Besides the usual seasonal events, there are concerts, fairs, carnivals, artistic events, movie nights and so forth. The purpose of the events is to raise awareness of the church and build a positive image of it. These events often serve as a way of easing a friend into contact with the church. Of the churches that had used more traditional events – such as Vacation Bible School or handing out the Jesus video – those experiences were generally not productive among the unchurched.

About half of the highly effective churches use some forms of advertising to get the word out, too. Most of that advertising relates to upcoming events. A few churches tried image advertising but could not justify the ongoing cost. Four out of five of the effective churches that tried radio advertising found it to be worthless unless it was to promote an event. "People don't go to church because of clever radio ads. They may attend an event, for an entertaining experience, based on an ad, but attending church is a different ballpark," reported one pastor.

The content of the worship service is crucial – but perhaps not in the ways usually assumed. To unchurched people, the most important thing they derive from their visit is a feel for the people, not the substance of the church's beliefs and doctrine. (A piece of research we did several years ago indicated that most unchurched people don't really listen to the content of the sermon that closely during their first two or three visits, but they scrutinize the delivery, the tone, the audience reaction, and both the speaker's and congregation's body language very carefully.)

The worship services, therefore, are designed to allow believers to truly connect with God, in a context that is culturally relevant and uplifting. The unchurched, who probably cannot distinguish authentic worship from a blueberry bagel, are scooping out the situation from their own, less-informed vantage point. So they notice that the music is fun but substantive. The dramas or videos are often humorous but poignant. The big-screen visuals make following and learning from the message lively and helpful. The sermon outline included in the program reinforces the importance of the message while also facilitating recall of the content. The Bible version that is used is a contemporary translation, with copies readily available to those who do not have a Bible with them. The length of the sermons, the topics addressed, the manner of presentation – all of those elements have been thought through to facilitate a dynamic presentation.

These churches are completely comfortable with allowing visitors total anonymity for as long as they want to remain undercover.. But once a visitor identifies herself as a newcomer a carefully conceived, multi-stage interaction process is triggered. In every service each attender is asked to fill out a response device of some type. Each church has a well-conceived and carefully carried out process once a visitor submits that information. The process itself differs from church to church, of course, but here is a fairly common approach:

1. The pastor or other church leaders are available to meet with visitors after the service in a designated area. There is no pressure to do so; during the service there is just a casual mention that these individuals are accessible.

2. Within 48 hours of attending the service, the pastor will send a letter of thanks to the visitor and encourage them to return and to call if they have any needs or questions the church can address.

3. Within 5 days of having attended the worship service someone from the church – often the pastor – will call the home of the visitor to again express their thanks for the visit, and to ask if they have questions.

4. If the visitor does not return, they continue to get mailings from the church, usually for at least a year and generally regarding upcoming special events.

5. If the individual returns a second time, then the church becomes more aggressive, either sending someone to the

person's home (big in the South, not as common elsewhere), or calling them, or sending another targeted letter. The idea at this stage is to get the person integrated into the life of the church, so they are invited to a newcomer's class. They are likely to receive several invitations during the next few weeks.

6. If the person attends the class, then a primary outcome is to get the individual involved in a service ministry.

We saw countless variations on this theme. There are special welcome or introductory dinners, home visitation and gift drop-off programs, e-mail messages, pastoral visitation, contacts by small group leaders, and so on. The most typical stream of activity though, is shown above.

One key to the process is getting the person involved as quickly as possible after they fill out a card. "We discovered that a lot of people won't fill out the card until they've been here three or four times," shared one pastor. "So we figure, OK, once you fill it out, that probably means you're ready to take the next step, and we want to make that easy for them. We make sure they get contacted several times in the next few weeks, nothing high pressure, just letting them know that we care, that we're available, that there are opportunities if they're interested." Why the rush to move them into a more intense connection with the church? Because most of these churches have learned that if a person is not integrated or connected to the life of the church through serving others or through a connectional ministry (e.g., class, small group), then the chances are very high of them not getting connected at all.

At the same time, this calls for deft judgment and patience. A church can easily become too aggressive and, no matter how well-intentioned, chase off an interested but cautious seeker. "We find a lot of people come once or twice or three times, maybe go away, then come back again in three or four months."

The associate pastor of a large church in the Cincinnati area added a key insight into why patience is an important factor in reaching the unchurched. "Becoming churched is a process, you know? So we try not to scare them off. We want them to feel like they can come back and try this place for as long as they like." He provided a key insight: becoming churched is a process, not an event.

There is a fine line between allowing people to get involved at their own pace and losing the window of opportunity. "Some people don't want to be pursued," we were told by one church leader. "There's a certain level of anonymity that is important for most unchurched people. In some ways, giving them the space to control the situation works well, but in other ways it obviously hinders our ability to follow up effectively. Sometimes they're waiting on us; other times, they're wary of us. It's hard to know what the proper balance is. We pray and believe God will guide us in these instances."

Most of the pastors we interviewed stressed the significance of the assimilation process. Merely getting people to attend services or become members, or even make a commitment to Christ was not deemed to be a sufficient outcome. "We feel like we have six weeks to connect them with somebody or else they'll drift away or stay in the shadows," was one comment that represented the feelings of many. "We try to get them into the life of the church as fast as they're moving, you know? We don't have a timetable for that; we're trying to be both patient and not negligent. We try to hit that balance by offering encouragement, direction and opportunities. At the same time, we try not to coerce or pressure them."

One of the most obvious conflicts that have gripped these churches is that between attraction and assimilation. "Our ability to attract people far outstrips our ability to minister to them in deep ways," admitted one pastor. "I just can't seem to train people fast enough to keep up with the demand. The more successful we are at reaching the unchurched, the bigger the challenge we have in developing mature followers." This problem seems to become more pronounced the larger the church gets. The leader of a congregation of 6000 people described the paradox, "Our problem isn't attracting them, we've grown pretty fast. The problem is having structures and seeing people get involved and looking after them. We don't feel we can slow down the front end, so what are we going to do? Hang out a shingle that says 'Sorry, we're full. Everybody else, go to hell.' Can't do that! So you do your best as people come in and keep trying to improve your structures."

BEST PRACTICES: PRODUCTS

What does "success" look like at churches striving to reach the unchurched? Surprisingly, there was not a lot of agreement on this matter. The most common answers we received were the following:

- baptisms
- increased numbers of people in small groups
- more people involved in serving
- a high percentage of new members who are not joining by transfer
- people indicating they have accepted Christ as their savior
- consistent attendance at worship services
- completion of the newcomers class

I was intrigued by some of the factors that were not mentioned. For instance, not one of the pastors mentioned the percentage of people in the church who invite unchurched people (most of the pastors had no idea what that figure currently is among their people) or increased knowledge of the basic principles of Christianity. Perhaps this was an oversight on their part, or maybe they felt that those outcomes were subsumed under other outcomes they had already mentioned.

All of these outcomes, along with the handful of others that were mentioned, relate to transformation. A pastor from Nevada stated the goal most clearly. "Our church is successful when people come to know Jesus Christ as their savior and Lord, and when their lives are changed. If people's lives aren't being changed by an encounter with the Almighty God and their families transformed and their communities impacted, then we've not made a difference. At the end of five or ten years our community better have changed by our presence or else I will really question the efficacy of what we've done. If it's simply a lot of people who said 'Yeah, I prayed the prayer' but their families didn't change and the community is not impacted, then I will really question the ultimate success of our mission here."

OTHER INSIGHTS GLEANED

In closing out this summary of what the most effective churches do to reach and retain the unchurched, let me relay eight additional bits of wisdom imparted by the pastors of these churches.

If your church is not attracting unchurched people, you're probably not ready to handle it. Although it is not a popular notion, sometimes churches fail to attract the unchurched because God is protecting both the church and the unchurched from exposure to each other. As we have seen, successful ministry to the unchurched takes more than just getting them inside the sanctuary. A pastor from upstate New York expressed this idea well. "God doesn't bring an increase if you can't handle it. If we're not prepared to take care of those who are evangelized, whether that's in the area of discipleship or getting them involved in ministry or whatever, God is too smart to bring the increase. Our job as church leaders is to put ourselves in positions where we're doing our part of the job. When numbers have slowed, in membership and conversions, that's always been a sign to me that something we're doing needs to be assessed and we need to prepare ourselves better for the next level of ministry."

If people start coming from other churches, that is a mixed blessing. If word gets around that your church is a special place, then you will probably start to attract many unchurched people – as well as many churched individuals. There are millions of Christians who habitually move from church to church, striving to be at the "hot" church in town. The influx of these people is generally a double-edged sword. On the one hand, their presence is a blessing because it is a sign that good word-of-mouth is happening on behalf of your church. Sometimes these people are mature Christians and can add value to your ministry, too. On the other hand, their presence is more often seen as a curse because they are more interested in being entertained or coddled than in growing and serving. The church typically runs a net loss in terms of ministry health as a result of their attendance because these people absorb more of the church's resources than they invest in the ministry.

You are not called to reach the world, only some portion of it. This statement will upset a number of people who interpret the Great Commission to mean that they are called to reach all non-believers. But that interpretation is neither accurate nor reasonable. Several of the pastors of the effective churches are cautious in how they use Matthew 28. One such pastor put it this way: "I want to be faithful to God's calling to me and to this church, but that calling is not for us to reach the entire world. That's the job of the Church worldwide. My immediate task is to try to share the gospel with every person near our church, though – and that's a daunting enough challenge. If I try to convince my people that we're supposed to win the entire world, they'll walk away, knowing that it's too big a challenge. But if I can give them a mission they can accept as reasonable – big, challenging, unprecedented, sure, but within the scope of reason – they'll climb on board." In other words, the challenges we pose to our people must be achievable.

Recognize that churched and unchurched people have similar needs and dissimilar needs. No, that's not double-talk. That is a

144

description of the magnitude of the challenge facing any church that straddles the fence between the churched and unchurched. We all have similar needs – love, comfort, security, belonging, food, clothing, shelter, etc. But the factors on which each group bases its selection of a church differ. Churched people are seeking a broad slate of strong programs along with challenging preaching and desirable music. The unchurched are searching for a grip on reality and personal applications. The churched want an organization of which they can be proud. The unchurched want relationships with people who are genuine and caring. The churched are seeking to improve their church situation. The unchurched are seeking to improve their quality of life. If you find the competing interests of these groups difficult to balance, know that you are not alone in the struggle, and that the problem is not likely to dissipate as long as you attract both groups of people.

The healthier your church is, the less of a problem "leakage" will be. Many churches that dabble in ministry to the unchurched become discouraged because so few of the visitors return and get involved. One secret to alleviating this problem is to be sure the people in your church are spiritually healthy. If they are, then they will have a heart for the unchurched and will aquire the tools with which to minister to them. If you reach many but retain few, evaluate the health of your congregants. In all likelihood you have a people problem, not a program deficiency.

Unsaved people can serve – and everyone can profit from the experience. Thousands of churches refuse to let unchurched people get involved in the ministry until they make a firm commitment to follow Christ. Most of the effective churches took a different stand. They had identified certain tasks that people could perform that enabled them to get involved, feel useful and encouraged them to attend more regularly. "You don't need to have accepted Christ to serve coffee or park cars or stuff programs," stated one pastor we spoke to. "I can't let them teach, but getting them to serve is a great step toward becoming a mature believer. I want to form that habit in them as soon as possible; letting them come and sit around, watching us do ministry every week is simply not healthy, even for a fence-sitter."

Standardized developmental tools are important, but not paramount. Frankly, I was surprised that a larger share of these churches did not use many of the resources and tools that have been created for use by churches. For instance, although many of these churches try to incorporate people into small groups as soon as possible, relatively few of the churches use the same small group materials. The Alpha course has been a viable tool for thousands of churches overseas, but only two of the effective churches use it, and less than a half dozen had even heard of it. The Internet is essentially an untapped tool; most of the churches had a web site, but nothing specifically geared to helping or reaching an unchurched person. Virtually every newcomer's class was based on self-developed materials. There was no standard procedure or materials used to gather information from people who visited and never returned. Yet, all of these churches are doing a terrific job. Maybe they could do an even better job if they used productive tools, but the lesson is certainly that impacting people's lives is dependent upon passion, prayer and people more than materials.

Ministering to the unchurched is serious spiritual business. As you delve into ministry to those who have little, if any, involvement with God, plan to encounter intense spiritual challenges. Strategically transitioning people from darkness to faith in Christ will stir up the powers of evil and generate stiff spiritual opposition. As the pastors of these churches indicated, you must be prepared to fight a difficult battle for the hearts, minds and souls of these individuals. Take Paul's advice and put on the full armor of God as you pursue the unchurched. Your ministry to them is a battle call to the enemy.

Eleven

COMMITMENT
TO A
VISION OF THE CHURCH

What are we striving to accomplish when we gather the saints and soon-to-be-saints together? Our goal must be more than just filling up the sanctuary or sustaining a menu full of ministry programs. This is where the importance of leadership comes into play. As you read through the book of Acts, it becomes clear that individuals emerged – Peter, James and Paul, for instance – who had been called by God to influence those who asked "What shall we do?" In the hearts and minds of those appointed individuals – His chosen leaders – He instilled a vision of how to move forward with the development of the Church. That vision is His blueprint for what we may do to experience the fullness of the life He gave to us.

If you are a leader called by God to move His Church forward, His vision is the cornerstone of your leadership. Communicate it clearly and persuasively to all who will listen, as often as you have the opportunity. Convey that vision in such a compelling manner that people can envision a future in which people's lives are being transformed to be more Christ-like, and in ways in which every individual can play a meaningful role. Pray for opportunities to share that vision, for people who will hear it and embrace it, for the resources to make it happen and for the ability to direct people's efforts efficiently and effectively.

If you are a follower of Christ but not called to such a leadership position, then listen carefully to the vision that is being cast by His chosen leaders and embrace the vision as if it were your own. Commit to it. Use your gifts and resources to fulfill it. Pray about the vision, about your role in bringing it to pass, and about God's willingness to use you in significant ways to reach the world for His glory. Listen and watch for His response to your prayers.

COMMITMENT TO PEOPLE

Strange as it may seem, God chose to work through human beings to glorify Himself. In my less profound moments – and they are legion! – I look at myself and other people and conclude that the creation of humanity was not one of God's inspired choices. But a careful read through His Word emphasizes that we are both an inspired and exciting creation. You and I have a chance to know the Creator intimately, and to be part of His kingdom, doing special works of service that He set aside for each one of us. What an incredible opportunity!

Analyze His exhortations to us and you will find that His challenges are all about how we work with people. Organizational structures and operational systems have a place in the larger scheme of things, but the reason for their existence is to build up people. Our energy must be poured into people.

But how can we do that in a meaningful way? There are so many needs, we easily get overwhelmed or sidetracked. What could we do to make a difference?

Working by ourselves, outside of a community of believers who are committed to a vision from God and taking direction from His chosen leader, perhaps we *can't* do much. That's why it's imperative that we work as a team – or, in religious parlance, as a church – to maximize our capacity to facilitate positive change in lives.

Of course, this sounds high-minded when described in such prosaic terms, but the reality is that being the Church that follows God's vision is all about the details of Scripture and change implementation. It relates to marketing, communications, training, fundraising, counseling, administration, and the like. Somehow those endeavors seem less holy and inspiring than talk about vision and the imitation of Christ. But they are one and the same; you can't get from here to there without such efforts.

Keep in mind our goal: it is not to build the perfect church, but to honor the perfect Creator. Our efforts must keep in mind our calling to worship Him, to know Him and about Him and His ways, and to serve Him and His people. The actual structure of the church does not really matter to God; if it did, He would have given us a detailed outline of what it must look like, just as He gave Noah exact measurements for the ark. But He didn't do that because He is more interested in the state of our hearts than in the size of our buildings or the design of our organizations.

GETTING "PRACTICAL"

If you're at all like me, the preceding paragraphs may seem like a preamble to the "real stuff" – the nuts and bolts of how we make the Church work. Without minimizing the significance of vision and teamwork and perspective, let me briefly address some of the details that may be part of the developmental process.

MODEL IT

Our research reveals a lot about the unchurched. Without question, their disinterest in the Church is partly because we have not adequately represented God. Once we clean up our act, our lives will become a pleasing fragrance not just to the Lord but also to those around us on earth. We may also help reduce their confusion by offering them distinctive options to pursue, such as churches that approach faith through different styles and emphases, but without ever compromising Scripture or ignoring the foundations of the church.

DISTINCTIVES

In our communications with them, remember that while relationships are important in building a church, the unchurched are a less relational group of people than the churched community. Relationships will only get us so far with this group. They still require a clear understanding of our USP – that's the business world's abbreviation for Unique Selling Proposition. In other words, what is it that we have to offer that is different and valuable in the eyes of the target audience? What they're looking for is a better life. They're not looking for a better afterlife. Can you lead them to a place or to a group of people that will deliver the building blocks of a better life? Don't position Christianity as a system of rules, but as a relationship with the One who leads the way by example. They are seeking proven ways to achieve meaning and success. Christianity provides that (and, along the way, redefines what those terms mean).

Keep in mind that as you describe that better life, and how well it has worked for you, the proof is in the experience: they don't want to hear about the Christian life or the joy of faith, they want to observe it in you and your churched colleagues.

Be on guard against making unrealistic claims. "Your life will never be the same," "you'll have a new family that loves you deeply," "you'll never be alone," "you will receive unimaginable power," "you've never experienced anything like this." No matter how true these assertions may be, they are not immediately credible (unless your life is a crystal clear demonstration of those very realities). Appeal to them in believable terms, and allow God to overwhelm them with His ability to deliver promises that are even bigger and better than we could ever make.

SUBSTANCE

We lose our opportunity to connect with many unchurched individuals long before they visit a worship service. The reason is because we have not read them well. They require control, independence and choices. In the church we generally require submission, not just to Jesus, but also to the dictates of the church. There is a natural conflict here – but it is not irreconcilable. If we are comfortable with, and confident in, our faith, are there ways that we can allow people who support liberal ideas, hyper-tolerance, and relativism to be in our midst, to hear and experience God's truths, without immediately stripping them of their predispositions? This is not a call to compromise, for that will bring defeat. It is a call to guide them into God's Kingdom through love, understanding, and diligence.

EXPLOIT ALL OPPORTUNITIES

It seems that we may not be taking advantage of all of the opportunities that are available to us. I am surprised by three conditions, in particular.

First, we do not seem to be exploiting the possibilities available through the Internet. Having a church web site is nice, but that's passive marketing – i.e., putting something on a site and hoping that those who need what you have will find it through some unpredictable and ill-defined search process. Are there more creative, aggressive and intentional ways of connecting with unchurched people to bring them into a deeper relationship with Jesus? Our research shows that a growing proportion of the population is open to, if not actively seeking, online opportunities to engage with God and His people. A church web site won't do it. Building a virtual church on the Internet may reach an entire segment of the unchurched that is otherwise inaccessible.

Second, I was also surprised by the predictability of the churches that are successfully reaching the unchurched. Without meaning to disparage any of those churches – they are doing a great job and the body of Christ is blessed by their presence and their example – I wonder if there aren't significantly different models of faith expression and community that could be created to reach this target market.

We know, for instance, that churched people are already clamoring for (and responding favorably to) new models of the church. The congregational format that we have used for hundreds of years in churches does not really fit our culture very well, so new models (house churches, marketplace ministries, cyberchurches) are attractive to growing numbers of people. Most of those models are being developed for disgruntled churchgoers. What would some new models look like for the unchurched? Who will have the courage to take the risk of experimenting with those models?

Third, it is surprising that we don't focus more energy on reaching children as our primary outreach thrust. Perhaps because we are adults it is our natural inclination to focus on people like ourselves. However, the research is very clear: people don't change much, they don't strive to change much and if Jesus is not already part of their lives by the time they leave high school, the chances of them accepting Him as their

Lord and savior are very slim (6%, to be exact). With children, it is just the opposite. Because of the challenges and insecurities they face in life, they are very open to being part of a community of like-minded people who grow together. We also know that children have tremendous influence within their families – on spending patterns, on entertainment choices, on relationships, and even on matters of faith.

Of the churches we interviewed that are most effective at reaching the unchurched, only one stated that their primary target group is kids. We did not speak to every church in America that is effective at reaching the unchurched; I realize that there are probably many other churches that do target kids. But the evidence suggests that we typically think about adults first, and assume the kids will tag along. Perhaps the reverse strategy would be true: a more concentrated effort at reaching kids would bring more adults (i.e., their parents) along for the ride. In fact, a more targeted effort at reaching kids might revolutionize the future church, when these kids are grown and needed as the church's leaders. Rather than having to re-interest them in the Church, perhaps their experience during their formative years would result in a positive re-engineering of the church to incorporate their generation.

THE HEART OF JESUS

One section of the Bible often comes to mind as I think about the unchurched. It deals with Jesus' reaction to the crowds who followed Him, searching for hope and answers. The Bible repeatedly describes how Jesus had compassion for the people because they were needy and helpless - "like sheep without a shepherd."

If you're like me, you have no trouble keeping yourself busy from moment to moment. One consequence of having a jammed schedule is that I often lack that ability to see the crowd the way Jesus saw it, and to realize that Jesus has called each one of us, even me, to have compassion on those who are searching for meaning and purpose in life. My prayer is that I might have the heart of Jesus for those people. It is my prayer for you, too.

There are almost 100 million people living in our own country who are not connected to a church. Millions and millions of them are desperately seeking a meaningful faith connection. You know some of them. What will you do to meet their need?

RESEARCH METHODOLOGY

This book is based upon a number of research efforts related to the unchurched and churches that minister effectively to them. Here is an outline of the research projects conducted by the Barna Research Group from which the data in this book were derived.

SURVEYS AMONG ADULTS

All of the following were telephone surveys based upon nationwide random samples of adults living in the 48 continental states. The surveys were conducted from the Barna Research field center in southern California, and interviews were conducted on week nights from 5:00 to 9:00 p.m., on Saturdays from 10:00 a.m. to 6:00 p.m. and on Sundays from noon through 8:00 p.m. (all times listed are the times in the time zone of the survey respondent). Unchurched adults were defined as those who had not attended a church service within the past six months, other than for a special event such as a wedding or funeral.

	Completed interviews among the:	
Survey field dates	Churched	Unchurched
January-February, 1999	750	282
April-May, 1999	0	601
July-August, 1999	727	273
November-December, 1999	723	230
January-February, 2000	675	327
May-June, 2000	681	322

Surveys Among Pastors

In addition to interviewing churched and unchurched adults, we also spoke with two samples of senior pastors of Protestant churches. One survey was a national random sampling of 601 senior pastors, conducted by telephone during June and July, 2000. That survey was a representative sampling of Protestant churches and included questions pertaining to ministry to the unchurched.

The other study was among an elite sample of pastors and church leaders from congregations that have done an outstanding job of reaching the unchurched. The original sample list was developed from calls made to denominational executives, church consultants and analysts, and ministry specialists. From that list we then narrowed down the body of "qualified" churches to those who are doing unusually effective ministry among the unchurched. That was determined by assessing the percentage of unchurched visitors the church attracts and retains each year; the ministry emphasis placed upon reaching unchurched people; and the number of changed lives that have resulted from such ministry. This portion of the research was qualitative and non-statistical in nature, based upon extensive interviews and evaluations of the church's efforts to reach and relate to unchurched people. The churches involved in this portion of the research came from every region of the country; represented more than a dozen Protestant denominations, mainline and evangelical; and ran from as few as 175 to as many as 6,000 adults attending the church on a typical weekend.

Additional Research

This book draws on information from other surveys we have recently conducted, as well. Among them is a nationwide telephone survey of a random sample of 610 teenagers, conducted in October 1999. Allusions are made to research we conducted in 1990, 1993 and 1995 among the unchurched, using those data for comparative purposes. Each of those studies was a national telephone survey among a random sample of unchurched adults, ranging in size from 307 completed interviews to 602 completions among the unchurched.

BIBLIOGRAPHY

Barna, George. *The Habits of Highly Effective Churches.*
Ventura, CA: Regal Books, 2000.

———. *Growing True Disciples.* Ventura, CA: Issachar
Resources, 2000.

———. *The Second Coming of the Church.* Nashville: Word
Books, 1998.

———. *Evangelism That Works.* Ventura, CA: Regal Books,
1995.

———. *Never On A Sunday.* Ventura, CA: Barna Research
Group, 1990.

Barna, George and Mark Hatch. *Boiling Point.* Ventura,
CA: Regal Books, 2001.

Colson, Charles and Nancy Pearcey. *How Now Shall We
Live?* Wheaton, IL: Tyndale House Publishers, 1999.

Hoffecker, W. Andrew (editor). *Building A Christian World
View, Volume 1.* Phillipsburg, NJ: Presbyterian and
Reformed Publishing Company, 1986.

Krueger, Otto and Janet Thuesen. *Type Talk.* New York:
Delta Books, 1989.

U.S. Census Bureau. *Statistical Abstract of the United
States, 1999.* Washington, D.C., 1999.

ABOUT
GEORGE BARNA

George **Barna** is the president of the Barna Research Group, Ltd., a marketing research firm located in Ventura, CA. The company specializes in conducting primary research for Christian ministries and non-profit organizations. Since its inception in 1984, Barna Research has served several hundred parachurch ministries and numerous churches, in addition to various non-profit and for-profit organizations.

To date, Barna has written 29 books. His most recent works are *Rechurching the Unchurched*; *Growing True Disciples*; *Effective Lay Leadership Teams*; *Boiling Point*; and *The Habits of Highly Effective Churches*. Past works include best-sellers such as *The Frog in the Kettle*, *The Second Coming of the Church*, *User Friendly Churches*, *Marketing the Church* and *The Power of Vision*. Several of his books have received national awards. He has also written for numerous periodicals and has published more than two-dozen syndicated reports on a variety of topics related to ministry. His work is frequently cited as an authoritative source by the media.

Barna is also widely known for his intensive, research-based seminars for church leaders. He is a popular speaker at ministry conferences around the world, and has taught at several universities and seminaries. He has served as a pastor of a large, multi-ethnic church and has served on several boards of directors. He is the founding director of The Barna Institute, a non-profit organization dedicated to providing strategic information to ministries.

After graduating summa cum laude in Sociology from Boston College, Barna earned two Masters degrees from Rutgers University. He also received a doctorate from Dallas Baptist University.

He lives with his wife Nancy and their two daughters (Samantha and Corban) in southern California. He enjoys spending time with his family, writing, reading, playing basketball and guitar, relaxing on the beach and visiting bookstores.

ABOUT THE BARNA RESEARCH GROUP, LTD.

The Barna Research Group, Ltd. (BRG) is a full-service marketing research company located in Ventura, California. BRG has been providing information and analysis regarding cultural trends, ministry practices, marketing and business strategy, fundraising, worldviews and leadership since 1984. The vision of the company is to provide Christian ministries with current, accurate, and reliable information in bite-sized pieces and at affordable prices, to facilitate effective and strategic decision-making.

BRG conducts both quantitative and qualitative research using a variety of data collection methods, with particular emphasis upon the application of the results. The company conducts more research within the Christian community than any other organization in the U.S. and regularly releases reports describing its findings regarding the values, attitudes, lifestyles, religious beliefs and religious practices of adults and teenagers, as well as the current state of churches. That information is also accessible through the seminars, books, website and tapes produced by BRG.

To access many of the findings of BRG, visit the company's web site at www.barna.org. You will have access to the free bi-monthly reports (*The Barna Update*) published on the site; a data archives that provides current statistics in relation to forty aspects of ministry and lifestyle; the various resources produced by George Barna and the Barna Research Group; and information about upcoming seminars as well as the firm's research activities. If you wish to receive *The Barna Update* by e-mail every two weeks, you may sign up for that free service on the home page of the site.

To contact the Barna Research Group, call 805-658-8885 or write to 5528 Everglades Street, Ventura, CA 93003.

ABOUT THE
BARNA INSTITUTE

The Barna Institute was founded as a not-for-profit, 501(c)(3) corporation in 1995 (originally named the American Perspectives Institute). Started by researcher George Barna, the organization was initiated to provide Christian ministries with strategic intelligence that would enhance decision-making and ministry activity. By supplying strategic information concerning key issues, conditions and opportunities about which ministries lack necessary insights, The Barna Institute intends to help ministries be better informed about the culture and people they are seeking to influence, resulting in more productive and life transforming ministry.

The Institute provides information that is otherwise unavailable to churches and Christian leaders by focusing either on topics that other researchers have not studied (or have not studied sufficiently) or upon topics that are too large for churches and other ministry organizations to independently fund. Past projects have included a study of the role of faith and churches among blacks in America; and the emergence of the cyberchurch and its affect on the nation's faith.

For more information about The Barna Institute, or how to become a Barna Associate, call 770-909-0000; write to The Barna Institute, 7657 Briar Crest Court, Riverdale, GA 30296; or e-mail us at barnainstitute@mindspring.com.

About The Barna Institute

166